———————— I shed the tear
For the dear *Manes*, that lie sequestered here.

Page 16

THE

LAST OF HIS FAMILY;

AND OTHER

POEMS,

OCCASIONAL AND MISCELLANEOUS

BY NATHAN LANESFORD FOSTER.

FOURTH EDITION, WITH ADDITIONS.

PHILADELPHIA:
PUBLISHED BY THE AUTHOR.
1850.

J. FAGAN, STEREOTYPER.

PREFACE.

Most of the poems which compose this volume have already appeared in various periodicals, and been favourably noticed. Prompted by the advice of a Reverend and much esteemed friend, who had read with approbation many of these poems, as they from time to time appeared before the publick; and also by a laudable desire to minister to the wants of a numerous family, dependent on him for support; the author is induced to commit this volume to the press; believing that it is as honourable to traffic in the *products* of the *brain*, as in the *goods* and *wares* manufactured by the *hands*.

In presenting these poems, in their present form, to an enlightened and discriminating community, the author does not aspire to poetical eminence.—For, should any degree of desirable distinction attach to him in consequence of their publication, he may not even hope to live long to enjoy it; conscious that his day of probation is near its close.

From candid reviewers, who are not strangers to sensibility and refined feeling, he has nothing to fear. Nor can the strictures of the self-constituted critick, nor any thing earthly, deprive him of the pleasure he has already enjoyed in writing some of these effusions; which, he has the happiness to believe, breathe the spirit of piety and devotion, which will be duly appreciated by the true disciple of the meek and lowly Saviour. The *sentiments* contained herein, —none of which, it is believed, can reasonably offend any denomination or sect, in religion or politicks,—the author fearlessly avows. With regard to the *dress* in which these sentiments are clad, he only desires it may be viewed with the eye of candour, and not be *rent* with a *ruthless hand.*

N. L. F.

Philadelphia, June, 1841.

PREFACE

TO THE SECOND EDITION.

GRATEFUL for the generous patronage which has enabled him to dispose of his first Edition of ONE THOUSAND COPIES, in the brief space of one year; and encouraged by the very courteous manner in which his humble production has been noticed by several Editors of distinguished piety and erudition, the Author is induced to publish a SECOND EDITION, enlarged and improved.

He indulges the hope, that his effusions may continue to receive the favourable notice of the religious community; and, especially, that they may meet the approbation of his DIVINE MASTER; — that his OCCIDENTAL SUN MAY SET IN A PACIFICK WAVE!

THE AUTHOR.

Philadelphia, December, 1842.

CONTENTS.

THE

LAST OF HIS FAMILY.

"*O! who would inhabit this bleak world*, alone!"

Visions of early life! how rise with joy!
When Love Maternal clasped her youngest boy!
How float ye o'er awakening Memory's gaze,
And picture scenes, light with prismatick rays!
The light of heaven first struck my infant sight,
Where, round the household, every scene was bright;
Where Love parental round its offspring twined,
And fondly trained for Heaven the nascent mind;
Where Love connubial warmed the parents' breast,
And *five* loved children those dear parents blest.
That Sire, ordained to guard religion's shrine,
Priest of the Cross, in panoply divine,
Dispensed, each Sabbath, Life's vivifick word,
And plead the cause of his ascended Lord.
So, o'er his dome the holy influence ran,
And taught the wondrous love of God to man.

Thus each young mind was early led to know,
That lasting comforts from Religion flow.

Ye scenes of happiness! too bright to last!—
Soon was this day with gloomy clouds o'ercast.
Firm health, which erst had cheered that loved domain,
Was soon supplanted by disease and pain:
Death sought his victims:—with resistless art,
His minister, ***Consumption***, aimed the dart!

Oh! hast thou seen the gay, the lovely flower,
Trampled and withered in a luckless hour?
In Flora's bright parterre, the pride and joy,
Snatched by the ruthless hand of truant boy?
Or, if transplanted to a richer soil,
Its glories fade, in spite of culture's toil?
—See, see, removed to yonder sea-girt Isle,
One lovely FLOWER!—[1]Fond parents' prayers, the while
In ceaseless strains—with sisters', brothers' sighs—
Poured ardent forth, to—***hold her from the skies:***—
She walks yon strand—she sails the Atlantick wave
In hope forlorn, to elude the impatient Grave!
While on her cheek, where beauty's vermeil rose
Once proudly blushed, the livid hectick glows;
And the fell flatterer, with insidious art,
Securely twines around the vital part!
Lured by false hope, behold her Father come,
Once more to bear her to her much-loved home.

But ah, what words—what limner's magick art,
His look can paint, or speak his anguished heart,
When first his eyes his drooping daughter view!—
He stands aghast!—the event his fancy drew.—
—She lives to reach her home. That altar stands,
Where erst her youthful heart, in Hymen's bands,
Was given to one, who now, in misery's doom,
Must light with Hymen's torch her early tomb!
—So dies ELVIRA! but no words can paint
The endearing graces of that early saint!
So dies *Elvira!* thus *Lysander* mourns,
While in his heart the Love of JESUS burns,
Whose minister he is,—and seeks relief
In duty's path, to quench his smouldering grief!

The next in order—lo! that MOTHER lies
On yonder couch,—impatient for the skies.
—"My dear, my loved *Elvira* led the way;
She greets my advent to the realms of day.
I fear not Death: my Saviour smooths my bed,
While on his breast I lean my aching head!"
Thus faith in CHRIST dispelled all vain alarms;
And thus MY MOTHER slept in JESUS' arms!
—I then was young:—but, oh! that death-bed scene
Shall never fade, though ages intervene.
My *Mother* dead!—at thy loved name, the tear
Unbidden flows, as at thy funeral bier!

Thy loss no earthly solace can supply;—
To mourn, is vain:—to live, is—but *to die!*

ALMEDA—lovely, youthful, blooming bride!
Thy lot comes next:—Again the whelming tide
Of anguish swells!—like *Samiel's* poisonous breath,
Consumption breathes, and blights this flower in death!
—Thou dear companion of my early youth,
Clad in the vestments of unvarnished truth;
Whose spotless mind embodied every charm,—
Whose heart, with sympathetick fervour warm:—
With every tie, to souls congenial, dear,
We could not hold you in this nether sphere.
By the safe-conduct of Religion's ray,
You left your friends and soared to endless day!
In yon enclosure of romantick graves,
(New England's loveliest stream whose margin laves,)
I saw *Leander* place thy covering sod,
And, in his anguish, cast his cares on GOD!

Inspire my Muse, Thou SOURCE of LIGHT divine!
As I approach my FATHER'S sacred shrine.
My reverend Sire—Instructer, Guardian, Friend!
Though not permitted on thy hearse to attend,
Thy *orphan child* shall ne'er forget that day,
When thou wast summoned from thy flock away.
Though the companion of thy youth had died—
Though of thy children none were near thy side—

Yet friendship's ministerings thick clustered round,
And 'mid thy lambs full many a friend was found.
If on the couch of death a boon attends,
Next to the Saviour, 't is the love of friends.
—Hear that dear *sister of the Church* inquire,
If friendship's hand can any hope inspire?
He sees affection's tears suffuse her eyes—
"Weep not for me"—the dying saint replies:
"That hope I long have cherished, still remains
"An anchor to my soul;—and mortal pains,
"Though now they rack this tenement of clay,
"Insure me comfort in the realms of day.
"A rest remaineth for the child of God,
"Who here in patience bears his chastening rod;
"For this assured REST, I long—I pray—
"And hail release from this encumbering clay."
—In the sure hope, immortal bliss to gain,
This *Christian Pastor* rests from mortal pain.

And now my *Brother!* nearest me by birth,
My *only one*—companion of my mirth—
My first associate—brother, friend, and guide,
Twined in whose heart, I sought no friend beside:—
How tranquilly our youth, our childhood ran,
Till time had led us to the state of man.
My fortune led me through fair science' ways;—
Thee, Glory called to win the warrior's bays.

And while me, *Alma Mater* nursed with care,
Thine was the lot the chance of war to share.
On bright *Champlain*, 't was thine to find a bed,
And blend thy graceful form with the promiscuous dead!
Thy requiem rose in martial musick's strains,
As moved thy corse o'er fierce Bellona's plains,
The rites were paid, without thy kindred near,—
Thy dust was hallowed with the stranger's tear!
—And though no marble indicates thy grave,
Where thou reposest, 'mid the unhonoured brave;
Posthumous praise, nor monumental stone
Could do thee justice, where thy worth was known.
A warmer heart ne'er glowed in human breast,
Nor nobler spirit mingled with the blest!

One more remains—my *Sister*, eldest born,
To twine with mine a heart with anguish torn
A few short years we sympathized in grief;
But soon *Consumption* came to her relief.
For, oh! what sweet release appears in sight,
As Faith unfolds to view the realms of light;
Where saints adoring tread the blest abode,
And hymn the praises of their Saviour, God!
Oft had she mourned her friends—her children slain,
And borne, with patience, sickness, grief and pain.
But now reclining on the bed of death—
In form emaciate—with laborious breath—

I found this dear one!—But no speech can tell
What heavenly raptures in her bosom swell!
Her cares are cast upon her Saviour's breast,
With anxious longing for the last behest—
"Come, faithful Daughter, of my Father blest,
Dismiss thy pain, and share the promised rest."
What heavenly visions burst upon her sight!
She sees, unveiled, the glorious realms of light:—
The host redeemed, with songs of ceaseless praise,
Around the throne their *Alleluias* raise!
She longs—she pants, their radiant choir to join,
And swell the strain of harmony divine.
What slender tie her gentle spirit holds!
What fragile tenement her mind enfolds!
—The moment came:—With ardent love I pressed
That faded form on this fraternal breast;
With eyes unpraised, she seemed to pierce the sky,
Like proto-martyr Stephen, near to die.
While, thus, celestial visions blest her sight,
The gentle spirit winged her heavenward flight!
That peaceful soul forsook her frail abode,
And sought the embraces of her Father, God!
—Here, though I praised Immanuel's boundless Grace,
That gave her victory in the Christian race,—
Here—first, the gloom of darkness shrouds my soul,
As this *last Sister* to her earthly goal
With speechless grief, reluctant, I consign;
And wish—and pray—*her grave* were also *mine!*

On her cold lips one ardent kiss I pressed,
And longed with *her* to enter into rest!
—AMANDA gone!—thus, falling one by one,
Have my loved kindred, ALL, their journey done.
AMANDA *gone!*—how truly I remain
LAST OF MY HOUSE—*with all my kindred slain!*

Yes—I remain ALONE! I tread the strand,
Where stopped my Fathers, from their father-land:
I walk, *alone*, New England's rugged soil,
The rich bequest of our Forefathers' toil:
I breathe, *alone*, her health-inspiring air,
And, lingering, pour my *solitary* prayer!
Long o'er my desolation have I wept,
And, whelmed in grief, my midnight vigils kept!
As o'er these ruggêd realms I shed the tear,
For the dear ***Manes***, that lie sequestered here,
With joy I view my wasting flesh decay,
As the precursor of a happier day,
When, with my Parents, Sisters, Brother,—all,
Around GOD's Throne I shall, adoring, fall!

Ye guardian Spirits of my Kindred, dead,
Watch o'er my path; surround my dying bed!
And, with commission from the FOUNT of LOVE,
Convoy my parting soul, to your bright seats above!

Mt. Parnassus, Con. Aug. 30, 1837.

POEMS;

OCCASIONAL AND MISCELLANEOUS

THE VERNAL MORN.

Bright Sol again yokes up his steeds,
  And drives the night away;
Eager I haste to range the meads,
  And hail the new-born day.

The woods and lawns invite to rove,
  The flocks the hills adorn;
The birds that carol in the grove
  Welcome the vernal morn.

The feathered choir, on every spray,
  Attune their notes to praise;
And to the glorious God of Day
  Their grateful accents raise.

The sportive flocks that climb the hill,
  The herds that range the vale,
The echoes of the murmuring rill,
  His genial influence hail.

2 *

"Shall man be mute while instinct sings,"
  Nor join the general joy?—
No; rather let celestial things
  His every thought employ!

Ye, who would rosy health retain,
  Arise, and shake off sleep;
Or you, with me, perhaps in vain,
  The lovely *Nymph, a fugitive*, may weep!

The breath of morn regales each sense,
  And cheers the languid frame;
Then, slothful sleep and slumber, hence!
  And hence, your sluggish train!

AURORA! still let me inhale
  Thy health-inspiring breath;
Oh, yet withhold me from the vale
  Of dread, *primeval Death!*

April, 1810.

TO MY FATHER.

ON HIS BIRTH-DAY; APRIL 8, 1812.

While clouds obscure the sky
And fleecy snow descends,—
My heart, with Friendship's sigh
Salutes my absent Friends:
My *Father* first; to him my soul draws near;
This day completes his fifty-seventh year.

My Brother, ever near,
My Sister, calm and mild,
Her lovely offspring dear,
My sainted-Sister's child—
Ye all will share the affections of my breast,
Till Reason's reign finds everlasting rest.

Nor absent friends alone
Monopolize my heart;
She, whose soft breast is prone
Connubial joys to impart,
Shall share my love—endear the tie of life,
Till nature groans in elemental strife!

MORNING HYMN.

Sweet the balmy breath of morning
  Sweeps along the dew-gemmed sward;
Let our hearts, mild grace adorning,
  Pour their matins to the Lord.

Early let our thoughts, aspiring,
  To all nature's God ascend;
Whose rich mercies, never tiring,
  On our wayward steps attend.

May our aspirations, votive,
  At His Throne acceptance find;
Of such vows, how strong the motive,
  To the Power who rules the *Mind!*

While our lips, in tuneful measure,
  Swell the hymn of grateful praise;
Let our souls—our richest treasure—
  To their Sire an offering raise.

GUARDIAN of our hours, nocturnal,
  THOU, to whom all praise belongs,
Let our voice, in strains diurnal,
  Chant Thy praise in choral songs.

While we sail life's stormy ocean,
  Let Thy mandate calm the wave;
Safely moored,—hushed each commotion,
  Sink we in the peaceful grave!

On the resurrection morning,
  Freed from dross—refined by love—
May our souls, rich Grace adorning,
  Claim Thy promised rest above.

HYMN.

SATURDAY EVENING.

How sweet the hour of calm repose,
That sets the mind from labour free,—
The twilight of the *seventh day's* close,—
That calls the thoughts, O God! to thee.

To Thee, my ravished heart aspires,
Whose hand directs my wayward feet;
Yet far too languid are its fires,
To raise to Thee an anthem meet.

When by-gone years pass in review,
And Thy paternal care I trace;
To Thee alone all praise is due,
Exhaustless Source of sovereign Grace!

Fain would my heart, with holy zeal,
Ascend the shining realms of day;
Low at Immanuel's footstool kneel,
And there my grateful offering pay.

But o'er earth's waste, 'tis still my doom,
Awhile to tread life's thorny road;
With this lone ray to pierce the gloom,
That I, at last, shall soar to God.

Yet, O how precious this LONE RAY,
Which rests our hope on JESUS' Love;—
A hope, that makes our darkness day,
And centres our desires above!

ELEGIACK LINES;

TO THE MEMORY OF MRS. ARPASIA EMMONS.

THOU *Muse* of Grief and Melancholy! come,
MELPOMENE, once more I ask thine aid,
Who erst hast deigned to guide my infant muse,
And to my thoughts elegiack fire impart;
Who erst hast led my youthful mind to pay
Her willing offering at thy mournful shrine!
Thou heavenly MUSE, thee I again invoke;
Once more descend and tune my sorrowing lyre.

My midnight lamp, with feeble, glimmering ray,
Almost designates the adjacent mound,
Where low in Death's embrace ARPASIA lies!
—'T was Heaven's high behest!—Then let her tomb,
Sad monument of youth's precarious fate,
Speak forth instruction, and engage the heart
Of her bereaved spouse. Methinks he cries—
And all her friends exclaim—" Relentless Death!

Thou lovest a shining mark—a signal blow!"
True: innate goodness dwelt within her heart;
At pity's call she lent a listening ear;
Her breast was ever warm with friendship's glow,
Humanity, benevolence and love:
She deeply cherished heaven-born sympathy—
That sympathy which feels for others' woes.
The private virtues,—conjugal attachment,
Maternal fondness, and a love of home
Were proudly her's:—But all could not avail
To stay the hand of death; for every grace,
That once endeared her to her friends on earth,
Endeared her more to her Almighty Friend.
—The spirit flies—"renewed in all her strength
And fresh with life—an offering fit for Heaven."
Her widowed husband mourns his absent Bride;
Her infant offspring, their maternal Friend!

But while we mourn ARPASIA's early doom,
Let not our grief be outward, "to be seen
Of men;" but "godly sorrow" let us feel,
Sanctioned by bland Religion's precious rules,
Which will our hearts correct, our lives reform,
And lead our thoughts to Heaven's Eternal King!

Let her bereaved partner long revere
Her dying counsel; let him ne'er forget
The pathos which enforced her *parting words*—

'Bring up our children in the fear of God,
Direct them in the blissful path to heaven;
Pray with and for them often: O, my friend,
This duty, I entreat, no more neglect:
Acknowledge your dependence upon God;
Invoke his holy name; implore his aid;
Observe Religion's ever blessed rules:
So shall you, here, enjoy his promised grace,
Hereafter shall partake his promised rest.'
—Monition blest!—A dying Friend's advice
Whoe'er forgets, *his heart must cease to feel!*
—Adieu, ARPASIA!—erst misfortune's child,
Thou yet didst freely share the earthly good
Which bounteous Heaven yields man. And now thy soul,
"Burst from the thraldom of encumbering clay,
"And on the wing of ecstasy upborne,"
Ascends, we trust, to mansions in the skies,
For ever to enjoy the promised rest.

February, 1815.

WILLIAM'S GRAVE.

ELEGY ON THE DEATH OF A SON; AGED FIVE MONTHS.

It is not the will of your Father which is in heaven, that one of these little ones should perish. JESUS CHRIST.

WHY heaves my breast with many a painful sigh?
Why glitters in my eye the frequent tear?
Why does my rebel heart almost complain
That Heaven calls home what Heaven was pleased to lend?

Fain would I bow submissive to thy will,
ALMIGHTY FATHER! fain 'be still and know
That thou art God;' fain would I bless thy name
That 'Thou didst give—that Thou hast taken away.'
But sure a GOD of MERCY will forgive
Our sighs, our tears, for *William's* early doom.

And is our lovely babe so soon recalled?
So lately lent us too—a blooming Flower—
To raise our hopes, then sink them in despair!—
—Alas, *the Flower fades!* But five short months

He blessed his parents' arms, ere he was called
To engage in conflict with the King of Terrors!
The conflict, how unequal!—ruthless Death,
The conqueror of kings and tyrants, strove
With feeble, helpless Infancy! yet vain
Was many a shaft;—the lingering victim lived
Through seven hours' conflict with the all-conquering Foe!
Till, racked with cruel pains, the lovely infant dies,
And to its Saviour's arms the new-born spirit flies!

Dear lovely Babe! torn from thy parents' arms!
To kinder arms received:—The Saviour said,
'Permit these little ones to come to me;
'For sure, of such is Heaven's kingdom formed.'
This blest assurance, though it gives relief,
And yields a balsam to the wounded heart,
Has not a power to check Louisa's tears.
My own poor heart, oft torn with kindred griefs,
Now bleeds afresh: (a Father's heart must bleed
O'er his dear infant son's untimely grave!)
It bleeds afresh, when accents such as these,
The overflowings of a feeling heart,
Assail mine ear—"*My son! my darling son!*
(My pale Louisa, sobbing, oft exclaims,)
"Ye, who have sons, can only know my fondness!
"Ye, who have lost them, or who fear to lose,
"Can only know my pangs! None else can guess them.
"A *Mother's* sorrows cannot be conceived

"But by a *mother*;—whose affections reign
"Without a rival, and without an end." *
LOUISA mourns her little *William* dead!
Louisa's griefs, *Louisa's* tears, are *mine* . . . .

Let *stoicks* smile—let *Cœlebs* feign a sneer:—
But all the genuine peace and happiness,
Which dwell on earth, dwell with congenial souls,
And *kindred minds* insure *connubial love.*
The sympathy of those, who *cannot feel,*
I do not ask, and sure cannot expect:
They, who *can feel,* accord the boon, unasked.

Oft have I shed the tear for others' woes,
And shared with them in sympathetick grief:
Frequent have I invoked the sacred NINE,
To give my moral song poetick dress:
Oft, in funereal garb, *Melpomenè*
Has decked the efforts of my infant muse,
Designed, by bland philanthropy, to assuage
And blunt the acumen of another's woe,
Correct the thought, and give a moral bent
To each volition of the feeling heart.
Let, then, each feeling heart reciprocate
That sympathy, so oft by me expressed;
That fellow-feeling, whose benign control

* Hannah More.

Can aid the oblivious hand of time to yield
A consolation to the bleeding heart,
And mitigate the poignancy of grief!
But let none mock my misery: let none,
Who have not, by experience, known bereavement
And mourned the loss of friends *as dear as life*,
Insult my sorrows, and enhance my griefs,
With proffer of condolence—falsely named—
More cold than Zembla's ever-during snows!
They truly *feel*—they, who alone survive
Their dearest friends all slumbering in the tomb!

Before my *William* died, methought I'd passed
Through all the sad variety of grief:
But now one 'nerve where agonies are born,' *
Whose keen vibrations I had never felt,
Is 'waked' for me!—Parents and kindred all—
(Save one loved Sister,) all, endeared to me
By ties of consanguinity, have paid
The debt to nature due. Oft have I wept—
Oft have I mourned—oft has my heart been riven.
Oft Death has sported with the dearest ties
Which bind my soul to earth. But ah! one pang,
Before unfelt, was still in store for me!
—Father of Mercies! pardon my repining:
Full well thou knowest how weak our nature is;

* They wake the nerve, where agonies are born!—Miss Seward.

How prone we are to grieve thy righteous Spirit;
How prone to murmur at thy wise behest!

To trace the mazes of thy Providence,
Is far beyond our ken. How very rare
Short-sighted man can see, that thou permitt'st
All seeming evil for some latent good.
Still must our reason own the important truth,
That *all thou dost*, is *right:* that good and ill,
That mercies and afflictions, all, are sent
To man, in love and kindness infinite,
In strict accordance with thy sacred will.

O, teach us, then, THYSELF:—our duty teach:
Give us contentment with our lot in life,—
A firm belief that all thy ways are just;
Thy grace impart to guide us in the way
That leads to Life. O, may we bow to Thee,
And wait prepared for thine Omniscient call.

October, 1817.

HUMAN LIFE.

Summam nec metuas diem, nec optes.—MARTIAL, v. 47.

WHAT scenes of woe obtrude upon his gaze,
As MAN walks onward through the devious maze
Of chequered Life! How oft his heart is rent
With fearful ills, by Heaven in mercy sent!
Here, tottering age is sentenced to the grave;
There, graceful youth—no human power can save:
Here, helpless infancy in anguish lies,
Mocks parent-fondness, and reluctant dies!
There, love connubial, with anguish torn,
Consigns a partner to Death's lurid bourn!—
All ties of nature feel the afflictive rod,
And yield, reluctant, to the hand of GOD!

O, when will proud, short-sighted, erring man
Aright the counsels of the ETERNAL scan?
To second causes ever prone to trace
Those seeming ills, which spring from sovereign Grace,
Obscured by darkness, whelmed in mental night,
Man scarce can own the ways of Heaven are right!

What lines of difference, traced in bold relief,
Mark HUMAN LIFE—commingling joy and grief!
What vast gradations, from the Imperial throne,
To the poor captive, doomed to toil and groan!
Yet, what lorn vassal, destined here to toil,
Would, with the proudest lordling of the soil,
Exchange condition?—Each, to *self* confined,
To the o'er-ruling HAND *of* ALL is blind:
And *all*, with most harmonious accord,
Repine at *fate*, and "fret against the Lord."

Were human minds endued with power to scan
The matchless wisdom of the Almighty plan;
Trace each effect to its unerring Cause,
And wisely read JEHOVAH'S equal laws;—
Man, then, might bow to His supreme behest,
Trust in His grace, and on His mercy rest.

Nor does he, darkling, rove this nether sphere:—
A lamp to guide—a light of Heaven is here.
Religion's light, the glorious Gospel's ray,
Illumes his path, and makes his darkness day:
God's holy Book expands before his eyes:
Man, if he will, may seize the heavenly prize!

But what can *Faith*, devoid of *Works*, avail?
A shoreless sea—a barque without a sail!—
What is *profession* but a fleeting breath,
If *practice* bind us in the thrall of death?

Profession holds the laws of Christ most dear;
Should not our practice, then, those laws revere?
—But see how deeds of hell deform the earth;
How vice and lawless passions spring to birth!
Here groans the slave—oppression wields his rod,
And "Nature wrong'd, appeals to Nature's God!"
Fair LIBERTY! is *this* thy boasted land?—
Where sons of Afric groan beneath the hand
Of ruthless tyrants; who, with CHRISTIAN name,
Traffick in human flesh, nor feel the shame;
And down to earth in hopeless misery bind
Each noble effort of the immortal mind!

WAR'S fiendlike spirit still stalks o'er our land,
And spreads destruction with his hellish brand;
Sports with the dearest ties of human life,
And whelms the world in misery and strife.
Reckless of widows' groans, of orphans' tears,
His blood-stained banner still the fiend uprears;
His iron car sweeps o'er the embattled plain,
While VIRTUE mourns, and MERCY pleads in vain!

O then, bless'd Spirit! source of Love divine,
On erring man in pure effulgence shine;
Illume his mind with thy celestial ray,
And gild the midnight darkness of his way;
Teach him to bow submissive to thy rod,
And own the rightful sovereignty of God!

DEDICATION.

WRITTEN IN A YOUNG LADY'S ALBUM.

Here, in this Book, devoted to the Mind,
Be treasured all that 's rich in Wisdom, Wit,
Religion, Virtue, Sense, Morality,
And all the sweets of scientifick Loro.
Here let young Genius strew his richest flowers
Glittering Castalian dews. Let Fancy wake
Her liveliest note, and charm the ravished ear;
Nor ev'n, if reason guide her heaven-ward flight,
Repress Imagination's daring wing.

Let all conspire to furnish ample store
Of intellectual food; on which the Soul,
Conscious of her high birth and destiny,
May feast, fearless of ill; and sure to find
A banquet fitted for a guest from Heaven.

The heaven-aspiring Soul no joy can know
So pure, as holding converse with her God.

Then let the votive strain, the matin lay
And vesper anthem, from the heart ascend,
In hymnick praise to all Creation's King!
Here, oft record thy gratitude and love;
Thy obligations own; thy sins confess;
Dependance recognise; thy faith inscribe;
Thy vows renew; and dedicate thy life
To Him, from whom each perfect gift descends.
So shall thy earthly pilgrimage be blest
With home-felt peace, which nought on earth can mar;
And Hope, that steadfast anchor of the soul,
Shall raise thy mind above the fear of death,
Illume the midnight darkness of the tomb,
And yield a foretaste of supernal joys.

TRIBUTE OF FRIENDSHIP.

TO THE RECTOR OF ST. JAMES'; NEW LONDON, CONNECTICUT, ON THE ANNIVERSARY OF HIS BIRTH.

Sweet is the memory of departed hours,
On whose brief date the ray of Friendship shone;
Long would I muse in retrospection's bowers,
Of joys to dream, and sorrows, once my own.
Mine once were joys: once *parents* smiled on me;
On me *fraternal love* serenely beamed:
Now, left bereaved of kindred, still I see
Bland *Friendship's ray*, which erst benignly gleamed,
Like Bethlehem's *Star*,—from gloom my heart to free,
And gain a meed, which Stoicks never dreamed.—
Kindness, disinterested, claims return:—
Shall not the *gratitude*, to Friendship due,
Like holy incense in my bosom burn,
Each year as on *this day* I think of you—
Eternal as the spheres their stated course pursue.

Lorenzo.

Nov. 9, 1817.

TO LORENZO:—WITH ACKNOWLEDGEMENTS.

(REPLY TO THE FOREGOING. BY THE RECTOR OF ST. JAMES'.)

While meteors blaze, or comets shine,
Friendship,—how sacred, how divine,
How holy, and how true!
Life's fires scarce burn without thy aid,
Sacred to solitude or shade,—
Lorenzo!—'t is thy due.

Thy peerless thought, thy faultless mind,
Immortal pleasure looks to find,
In a vain world like this:
Exiled to earth, man knows his doom,
His soul, escaped, survives the tomb,
And soars to worlds of bliss.

There, friendships pure, without alloy,
With rapture taste celestial joy,
And hail their peaceful dome;
Angels take up their tuneful lyre,
And consecrate each fond desire,
To happiness and home.

S. B.

TO LOUISA.

ON THE ANNIVERSARY OF OUR NUPTIALS.

YE sacred NINE! my heart inspire,
And warm me with seraphick fire,
While I record the pleasing lay—
"How sweet is Love's first gentle sway."

Ye hallowed transports of the soul,
Enwrap me in your sweet control;
And let your influence ne'er depart,
But fan the flame that warms my heart.

How oft the best affections wane;
How oft true love meets cold disdain!
How oft, alas! does time assuage
The fervour of the youthful age!

There are, who, when familiar grown,
The bond of wedlock would disown;
And seek true happiness to draw
From "freedom's love," and "nature's law."*

---

* O happy state! when souls each other draw,
When *Love is liberty*, and *Nature law.*—POPE.

How vain the search!—it is not found
By wandering o'er forbidden ground:
The endearments of a virtuous WIFE
Amalgamate the joys of life.

The sweetest transports of the mind,
The purest joys on earth we find,
Reside in the domestick scene,
Where prudence holds the "golden mean."

When fortune frowns—when griefs annoy—
When foes malign our hopes destroy—
At *Home*, in sympathy, we find
A solace for the enanguished mind.

A heart, by oft bereavements riven,
For comfort looks from earth to heaven;
A *bosom Friend* then points the way,
To regions of immortal day.

Thus, my LOUISA, let us share
Each other's joy—each other's care;
And, heart and hand, devoid of strife,
Walk calmly down the vale of life.

In christian hope, and humble zeal,
In joy or sorrow, woe or weal,—
Be ours that peace, whose joys divine
Are richer than *Golconda's mine.*

With confluent efforts to do good,—
Our pardon sealed in JESUS' blood,—
The purest joys to mortals given
Shall antedate our bliss in Heaven.

Then while we sail life's treacherous wave,
And journey onward to the grave,
Record, with me, the genial lay—
"How sweet is *Love's* perennial sway."

When Death, at last, shall bid us part,
Though nature groans, and bleeds the heart,—
May Faith in CHRIST dispel the gloom,
And gild the horrors of the tomb.

"Blest SAVIOUR! cheer that darksome way,
And lead us to the realms of day;
To milder skies and brighter plains,
Where everlasting sunshine reigns."

May 30, 1824.

MEDITATIONS.

WRITTEN AT MIDNIGHT,

WHILE WATCHING BY THE COUCH OF TWO CHILDREN WHO WERE ACCIDENTALLY SCALDED.

Deplorable indeed the lot of those,
Who human ills to *second causes* trace:—
A God there is,—omniscient, just, and good,—.
A great *First Cause*,—who all events controls.
Else, why should infant innocence be doomed
A prey to sickness, accident, and death?
A righteous Sovereign reigns!—a God of love,
Who chastens whom he loves.

On *these*, indeed,
The chastening how severe!—Weep not, *my babes*:—
Your heavenly Father sees, and feels for, you.
" Suffer the little children," Jesus cried,
" And ne'er prohibit them, to come to me;
" Because, of *such* is Heaven's kingdom formed."

Emblems of Innocence!—Oh, sleep, my babes!
Sweet sleep, at length, has deigned to seal your eyes;
But ah! too oft a groan proclaims your pain!
Yet you complaint not—nor need you complain;
For God to the "shorn lamb tempers the wind."
But why thus suffer?—ye no crimes have known;
No sins have yet defiled your spotless hearts.
—O, for a state like yours! ethereal, pure,
Primeval innocence—devoid of fear.

Lo! fruits 'of man's first disobedience'—
Disease, misfortune, accident, and death,
And all the train of ills, ordained for man!
How thick they spread our path; how oft infuse
The bitterest dregs in pleasure's sparkling cup!
—With brightest ray, rose, erst, my morning sun;
But, long ere its meridian height it gained,
Dark clouds its beams o'ercast, and murky night
Obscured its glories in sepulchral gloom!*
Friend after friend, the shadowy vale of death
In quick succession sought. The stern behest
Of Heaven's all-ruling Sire, none may resist.
'T is thine, O man, to bow; the hand adore,
That lays thy glory prostrate in the dust!

---

* *The writer was left, in the morning of life, the sole surviver of his Family*

Severe the discipline, which to the foot
Of JESUS' cross my stubborn heart subdued.
Tie after tie, that bound me to the world,
Was riven, to form that holiest of ties,
Which binds me now to Him, who *wounds* to *heal*.

Afflictions, sanctified, are Heaven's best gifts.
Oh, then, Thou great ETERNAL! shower thy grace
On me, thy erring servant: bless my babes;
Preserve their lives; and may they 'walk in truth.'
And when, at last, Thou call'st us to thy bar,
May we possess that child-like frame of mind,*
Which our bless'd Lord assured us, *all* must have,
Who claim a mansion in the realms of bliss.

---

* St. Luke, xviii. 17.

THE AUTUMN BLAST.

"We all do fade as a leaf."

Sweeps by the Autumn blast;—
It seems the "knell of our departed hours:"—
Late, summer lingered o'er the blooming flowers;
Now Summer's bloom is past:—
Sweeps by the Autumn blast!

Sighs the lone evening breeze:
It is the dirge of Summer's beauty gone—
Beauty, that erst arose with Summer's dawn:
Hoarse, through the faded trees,
Sighs the lone evening breeze!

Alas! that faded leaf!
An emblem sad, of Man's uncertain date:—
So changing—fading—is earth's brightest state;
Man's longest day so brief:
Alas! that faded leaf!

Shall earth's gay bloom revive?
Though gelid breath of wintry winds deform,
Renascent Spring will renovate its form,
And new-born lustre give,
And earth's gay bloom revive.

The wintry blast of Death
Shall lay man's proudest glories in the tomb!
But Faith in CHRIST will pierce the midnight gloom;
And God's vivifick breath
Annul the power of Death.*

The *Resurrection* morn
Shall rouse the lowly slumberers in the earth;
And countless myriads, at this awful birth,
To deathless life be born,
On that refulgent morn!

CHRIST comes to judge the world!
The BLEST have robes made white in JESUS' blood; †
But, ah! the *scorners*, to the avenging flood
Must be for ever hurled,
When CHRIST shall judge the world!

---

* 1 Cor. xv. 26.

† Rev. vii. 14.

MONODY.

ON THE DEATH OF MRS. CHARLOTTE GREEN;

WIFE OF MR. RICHARD W. GREEN, OF PHILADELPHIA;

WHO DIED JULY 3, 1829

Respectfully inscribed to the surviving Parent and the bereaved Partner of the Deceased.

How deep thy counsels, thou ETERNAL SIRE!
Inscrutable to man!—Yet though our view
Kens not thy ways, thy JUSTICE, who shall scan?—
—Thou weeping *Mother*, dry the scalding tear;
The lovely Maid was thine:—Bless God who lent
That you might rear, an offering fit for Heaven.
Your task was finished.—The accomplished mind,
The graceful form, the intellectual fire,
And genius angel-bright, as with a zone,
Enshrined the blooming Fair one.

These rich gifts
Endeared her to the circle of her friends.
Death, too, they charmed: he "loves a shining mark,

A signal blow." But beauty, wisdom, wit,
No more than gold, can bribe him. His the task
To ope the gate, which simultaneous pours
The flood of *grief* on stricken kindred left,
And *joy* on saints released from "mortal coil."
Thou widowed ***Husband!*** hast thou yet to learn
The high behest of Heaven—'Be still, and know
That I am God!' * Though grief unknown before
Now rends thy heart, yet mourn not thou 'like those
Who have no hope.'—Cease thy threnodial strain,
And bless the bounteous Giver of all good,
That he hath blessed thy arms with such a bride:
That one short year of life's rough pilgrimage
Was solaced with endearments rich and rare.
Earth's richest treasures are most prized, when lost:
But what your loss is deemed, to her is gain;
And may prove gain to you:—not joyous now,
But grievously severe, the event may yield,
If you are duly exercised thereby,
Of righteousness the rich and peaceful fruit. †
This chastisement was doubtless requisite
To bow your stubborn heart, subdue your pride,
And bring you, suppliant, to IMMANUEL's cross;
And, while it brings conviction to your mind,

---

* Ps. xlvi. 10. † Heb. xii. 11.

By what frail tenure earthly joys are held,
To make you own—a RIGHTEOUS SOVEREIGN reigns!

While, then, you mourn your youthful bride laid low,
And in your heart's deep core her worth enshrine;
O, emulate her virtues: hold most dear
Her heart-warmed counsels and her stainless life:
Protect her *child*—pledge of your *Charlotte's* love,
Whose nascent life has caused your *Charlotte's* death.
The *parent's care* survives the *husband's love*:—
Take, then, this "softened image" of your spouse,
And train her up for heaven. Let *Charlotte's* name
Descend to her, and *Charlotte's* virtues too:
And as her infant mind expands to catch
The moral truths from fond paternal lips,
Teach *her to be* ALL that your CHARLOTTE *was*.

"Bear with me in my folly:"—I, too, feel
Her loss, and mourn her death. My *pupil* once—
A tie was formed, which pure affection claimed;
And, sundered thus, condolement fills my breast.

With fond delight, my memory dwells on days
Of by-gone years, spent in instructing youth.
The days which closed the week seem far most dear,
When labour ceased, and Sabbath's rest drew nigh.
Then, as my custom is, I fix the mind,
By serious lecture on Religion's truths,

Morality's requirements, and the chain
Of social duties; call the wandering thoughts
From earth-born cares, and lead them to the SAVIOUR.
To themes like these, your *Charlotte* listened oft;
And thus, (consoling thought!) an humble means
I may have been, in winning her to CHRIST.

Ask you condolence, now, *bereaved spouse?*
In christian sympathy, accept the boon.
No mockery is here:—I, too, have mourned;
Borne the disruption of the dearest ties
Which bind the soul to earth! Now left alone
On earth's wide waste! They, who have never known
Bereavement by the loss of dearest friends,
May *talk* of sympathy, but *feel* it not.

Ask you instruction?—that, too, I will give
In plain and homely words;—and you will hear—
You, erst my pupil too:—That faithful trait,
Which ruled your *Tutor's* breast, now sways your ***Friend.***
—There's "balm in Gilead—a Physician" there:
His voice of mercy calls *—"Come unto me,
"All ye that labour; I will give you rest.
"My yoke upon you take, and learn of me,
"For I am meek, and of a lowly heart;
"And everlasting rest your souls shall find:
"For easy is my yoke, my burden light."

* St. Matt. xi. 28, *et seq.*

ELEGIACK LINES.

OCCASIONED BY THE DEATH OF MISS. TEMPERANCE SMITH; WHO DIED OF THE CONSUMPTION AT EAST HADDAM, CONNECTICUT, JAN. 26, 1830. ANNO ETATIS XXIII.

Yes, she is gone !—How late the roseate hue
Of blooming health glowed sweetly o'er that face.
Strength graced her youthful step ; her mind was peace ;
The smile of conscious innocence illumed
Her countenance : the song, and converse blithe,
Spread joy around her. Hers the social gift
To grace the youthful circle. Filial love
Dwelt in her heart, and crowned domestick joy.

Another ornament—another grace
(Compared with which, all other graces fade,)
Was supervened. She saw—she felt—she owned,
That, without *Grace Divine,* all else was vain.
She sought—she found her SAVIOUR ; and with *him*
In *Jordan's* wave she laved.

High health was hers:
And youthful hope, alert, on buoyant wing,
And youthful expectation, swelled her breast.
Joyous anticipations rose to view;
But soon, alas! too soon to be deceived!
Her morning views how bright! Parental hopes
How ardent! Love fraternal round her cast
Its genial embrace. All loved, who knew,
All prized, who best discerned, her genuine worth.

Vain every grace; vain every virtue, here,
To stay Death's hand, or chain our joys to earth.
Earth's joys, how evanescent! frail their date!
The germ of dissolution hidden lies,
To foil our brightest hopes!

Here fell disease
Delayed not long his meditated blow.
The pale, *pale* cheek glowed with the *hectick flame:*
Consumption, slow but sure—Death's harbinger—
And *flatterer* false!—assailed the blooming form.
Now hopes and fears alternately prevail;
Parental love watched o'er her; anxious friends
And kindred daily viewed, with hope and fear,
These *ominous alternations*:—Faint the *hope*,
But almost sure the *fear!*—Yet, fear we—what?
That by her death we lose her:—not that she
Hath aught to fear—hath aught to lose:—her death
To her is gain. The soul, when ripe for bliss,

Is stinted here by earthly shackles. Death,
Though 't is an "awful theme to guilty man,
Is, to the saint, whose faith can pierce the veil
And see the crown of life which JESUS holds,
The welcome herald of immortal joys."
Supreme self-love alone could wish her stay,
When she herself,—though willing to impart
Whatever joy was yet within her reach,—
Could with composure view the approach of Death,
And hail him as the messenger of peace.
—Her hope was stayed on Christ: This hope alone
Above the fear of death can raise the mind,
Illume the passage through that gloomy vale,
And yield an antepast of heavenly joys.

Then let the self-deluded *Infidel*
And worldly *Moralist* approach this couch,
And see how calm, how sweet, the *Christian* dies!

Oh, may her early grave instruction give
To all who mourn her loss. Youth here may learn,
And hoary age grow wise.—Instruction blest—
Imparted from the confines of the Grave!
—Deny your SAVIOUR,—ye, who dare deny;
Depend on *morals*, ye, who Heaven defy!
Yet know, that nothing but IMMANUEL'S love
Can bear your spirits to the world above;
That *Faith* in CHRIST, alone, can cheer the way,
And hail you welcome to eternal Day.

HYMN TO THE SAVIOUR.

LET all the joys of earth retire,
  Devotion lend her sacred flame,
And pure seraphick thoughts inspire,
  While we invoke our Saviour's name.
Thou NAME adored, all names above;
  To Thee our hearts their anthems raise;
We hail thee, Source of boundless love!
  The object of our holiest praise.

What mortal powers can tell that Love,
  Which led thee from thy blest abode;
From the bright realms of bliss above,
  To dwell on earth—the incarnate God!
Thy precious blood in streams was shed,
  To purchase pardon for thy foes;
And crowned with thorns thy God-like head,
  To save us from impending woes.

What peerless Love thy bosom fired,
  When, nailed to the accursed tree,
Thy life in groans and prayers expired,
  From sin and death our souls to free.
Should universal nature raise,
  In loud acclaim one general choir,
How feeble all our notes of praise,—
  Inadequate an angel's lyre!

MIDNIGHT.

THOUGHTS, PENNED WHILE WATCHING BY THE BEDSIDE OF A BELOVED CHILD.

How solemn is this hour! It seems the sleep
Of universal Nature—deathlike rest!
A gloomy silence reigns, a solemn pause
That renders SILENCE *audible!* The form,
The pictured image of the sleep of Death,
Stands forth to view, at Midnight's fearful hour!

With pallid cheek, Death's semblance, MARY lies
In fitful slumbers. Ever and anon
She starts: and, exercised with pain, exclaims,
"Oh, I am sick! my head! my burning brain!"
—Art thou a father? Hast thou seen thy child,
Thy daughter, lovely, and too well beloved,
Stretched on the bed of sickness, racked with pain—
With fever burning—vainly wooing sleep?
And hast thou watched beside her midnight couch,

Witnessed her feverish pulse, her quick-drawn breath,
Her throbbing temples, her imploring eye?
Then, as a Father's love has prompted thee,
Hast thou let fall the frequent tear, and knelt
Beside her couch, as she unconscious lay,
And poured the fervent prayer, in hope to reach
The ear of Mercy, that thy child be spared?—
Hast thou done THIS?—then thou hast *felt*, and ***prayed.***

Yet what avails our feeling? what, our tears?
And what, the holy principle of love
And pure affection for the loved of earth?
These prompt humanity, indeed, and acts
Of kind attention, to impart relief,
To mitigate the pain, and calm the mind.
But vain are human help and human art,
To arrest disease, or stay the hand of Death!
But prayer—effectual, fervent prayer avails.
The prayer of faith can reach the eternal Throne
And move the world! 'Prayer, ardent, opens Heaven.'
'T is writ—"the prayer of Faith shall save the sick." *
—O, blessed promise! Holy Spirit, come;
Breathe thy divine *afflatus*;—warm my heart;
Inspire the ***prayer of faith.*** Oh, give me power
To call a blessing down. Thou righteous God!
Thou soul's Physician! minister thine aid.

---

* James, v. 15.

'T is thy prerogative to kill, or cure:—
Thou gav'st at first; on Thee all life depends.
To the shorn lamb thou temperest the wind:
To this *dear lamb*, thy heavenly grace impart;
Beneath her, place thine everlasting arm;
Support her sinking form; and bless the means
The healing art and *parents'* love supply.
Without thy blessing, vain are human means.
Oh! spare my child! remove the deathly hues
That blanch her cheek; restore the vermeil tints,
And let renascent health pervade her frame.
—Then, in review of thy restoring Grace,
Oh, let her dedicate herself to Thee,
A living sacrifice;—her heart and soul
Be wholly thine. Let child-like innocence
Mark her whole life;—and child-like purity,
Which can alone, as Christ hath said, win Heaven,
Secure her welcome to her SAVIOUR's arms.

THE VOICE OF FRIENDSHIP.

WRITTEN AFTER RECEIVING A VISIT FROM SOME DEAR RELATIVES FROM GREEN PORT, L. I.; OF WHOSE EXISTENCE I HAD BUT RECENTLY LEARNED.

WAKE! tuneful Harp, awake! My *Friends* demand
Thy feeble efforts ;—Friends, how dearly loved!
This lonely heart to bless, no Friends survived
Methought: but YE, as if *alive* from *death*,
Have come to bless these eyes, which long have sought,
And sought in vain, to find a *kindred soul.*
"Harp, lift thy voice on high," in hymnick praise
To God, the widow's Judge—the *orphan's* friend!

Ye came:—and renovated life once more
Hath warmed this widowed heart!—but ah, too short
Your stay: too soon, by far, ye bade adieu,
To hasten your return, and re-embrace
The *nearer friends* at home.

Well—go in peace;
And may the choicest benison of Heaven,
The Grace of GOD—IMMANUEL's precious Love—
Rest on you all!—While memory remains,
This unexpected meeting—this embrace—
This friendly visit—and this sad adieu,
Will thrill with joy—with pain—this feeling heart!

I envy not that heart of "sterner stuff,"
Which greets a friend, and bids him then depart,
Without emotion, and without a tear.
—God grant we meet again on this side Heaven—
Hold social converse, and recount the scenes
Of by-gone days! Here, on these rugged realms
If yet I dwell, may friendship guide your feet;
And may I yet salute your peaceful dome
On yonder sea-girt Isle; and there inhale
The sea-borne breeze, the health-inspiring gale,
That gently breathes your happy Island o'er.

There, in the bosom of that fertile Isle
Reposes *dust*, which claimed a kindred soul.
Near kindred of my kindred! where are ye?
One generation's gone—another comes—
But yet, in lineal line, blood of my blood—
Bone of my bone—and heart, and soul allied.
O, tell me all: tell how my *sister* pined,[2]
And by degrees *consumed* with fell disease:—

Tell where your Fathers, where your Mothers lie:
The great, the good, the Reverend Emerson—
The Minister of God—where lies his dust?
"On Brooklyn's heights," say ye?—and yet no stone,
No towering marble designates his grave!—
A Mausoleum his, in every heart
That knew his worth; and hearts no doubt there are
Yet warm with life, which vital food received
From him, who broke to them the bread of life.

But he is gone—and many a brother gone—
To his last audit, to receive the crown
Of righteousness,—the sure reward laid up
In store for faithful Pastors.

Then, my Friends,
Let us, their progeny, essay to walk
Their heaven-ward steps,—their virtues emulate,—
That we, at last, may join our feeble voice
With theirs, in chorus, round the Eternal's Throne!

Mt. Parnassus, Con.

HYMN FOR THE NATIVITY.

I SING the exalted Saviour's birth:—
What loftier theme exists on earth,
Or wakes the song in heaven?
Let ransomed man take up the song,
And swell the chorus loud and long,—
For Death's strong bars are riven.

Infinite Mercy formed the plan,
Thus to redeem rebellious man;
For this was JESUS born;
His heavenly Father to obey,
He left the radiant realms of day,
On this auspicious morn.

Oh, could we catch the thrilling strain,
That, floating o'er *Judea's* plain,
Announced IMMANUEL'S birth;
When the blest Star o'er *Bethlehem* stood,
And poured in living light its flood,
To bless the sons of earth.

Let the loud anthem pierce the sky—
"All glory be to God on high,
    And peace pervade the earth;"
Let our glad voices join the strain,
Which echoed through that seraph train,
    Who sang the Saviour's birth.

O, may this consecrated hour
Breathe in our souls devotion's power;
    And oh, thou Heavenly Dove,
Eternal Spirit! fire each heart,
To bear an humble, fervent part,
    In hymning JESUS' Love!

Dec. 25.

TO ELVIRA.[3]

"The heart that bleeds for others' woes
Shall feel each selfish sorrow less;
And HER, who happiness bestows,
Reflected happiness shall bless."

ALL hail, to the FAIR ONE, whose soul-warmed affection
My desolate state hath vouchsafed to bemoan;
A transport awakes at the dear recollection,
No solace of earth for whose loss can atone.

Dawns the ray of pure Friendship o'er yon azure ocean?
A *transient sensation* it never will prove:—
ELVIRA! *loved* NAME!—let the soul's pure devotion
Light up in our bosoms the incense of love.

Vain, specious, delusive, the bright coruscation,
If sense and stern virtue compose not its base;
Religion can chasten the heart's adoration,
And earth's dearest idols for ever efface.

May all we should treasure, and all worth possessing,
O'er your pathway in life, in profusion be given;
On your morn—your meridian—your evening—be pressing,
Resplendent with light, and with peace, and with blessing—
Encircle you here, and enrich you in Heaven!

[*This little poem is here with propriety introduced, as a prelude to the next succeeding. It is from the pen of a dear kinswoman and christian sister, now deceased; and of whom the reader of this volume will be again reminded.*]

LINES ADDRESSED TO * * *

Dearest, does Jesus' precious love
 Still fill thy heart with joy?
And do the pleasures of the world
 Seem like a trifling toy?
Does Bethlehem's star still lure thy gaze
 Upward to those fair climes,
Where warble songs from angel tongues,
 And Heavenly glory shines?

Ay, I rejoice, that thou art bound
 For Canaan's blissful shore,
Where sad adieus and farewell tears
 Are never heard of more.
Though I am distant far from thee,
 Still rises my warm prayer,
That thou may'st be the object of
 The Lord's peculiar care.

Oh may the banner of his love
  Wave sweetly o'er thy head,
Cheer every sad and lonely hour,
  And dry each tear that's shed.
May heavenly light illume thy way,
  And gild the scenes of earth;
May God's own spirit guide thy feet
  In wisdom's pleasant path.

Shun all the vain pursuits of life,
  Thou dear one of my heart;
And from thy Saviour's bleeding side,
  Oh may'st thou ne'er depart.
Sweetly glide on thy future years,
  Calm and untroubled too;
May hopes immortal fire thy soul,
  While journeying here below.

Yes, may Religion's tranquil ray
  Be ever on us shining;
While in this changing vale we stay.
  Where bliss and pain are twining.
And may our frail and tossing barque
  Arrive safe home at last,
To meet the loved and lost of earth,
  And mingle with the blest.

ELVIRA.

New York.

REPLY TO ELVIRA.

WHAT friendly voice, borne on the *Southern* gales,
With accents sweet, my raptured ear assails?
From yon proud City comes the pleasing strain,
And joys my heart—the accustomed seat of pain.
'T is thine, ELVIRA! name for ever dear,
At whose bare mention, flows the unbidden tear!
Name, erst, of ONE—mine by a nearer tie,
Removed, long since, to mansions in the sky!
A *sister* dear;—whose feeble frame enshrined
A soul of virtue, and a spotless mind.
—But why digress?—'t is not my aim to paint
The endearing graces of that early saint!
Of the same lineage, in THEE I trace
The lovely lineaments of her angel face.
And, as the mantle of *Elijah* came
On Seer *Elisha*, so let this loved name
Descend on thee; and me, thy *brother*, own,
Who, of that family, survive ALONE!

Yes, thou wilt own me; for 't is thine to feel—
Already glows thy breast with holy zeal:
Thou, too, hast felt th' Almighty's chastening rod—
With me, confidest in the *orphan's* God!
"Dearest, does Jesus' love still joy thy heart?"
Words cannot answer—words want power to impart,
To vision's organ, what that soul doth prove,
Made the recipient of Jesus' love.
Something must supervene, that soul to bless,
Beyond the powers of language to express:
Thoughts, feelings, sentiments, each sense control,
And fill with ecstasy the ravished soul!
Description languishes, and words expire—
We need an angel's tongue—a seraph's fire;
Yet, useless were it, with such powers if blessed,—
A soul like thine can read them unexpressed.
Thou feel'st and own'st Religion's bland control,
And seest its radiance in a kindred soul.
Dearest, with thee I 'm bound to Canaan's shore;
With our endearments death shall sport no more.
Tears and sad farewells in that clime shall cease,
And the rapt soul will rest in conscious peace.
Yet while we sail on life's tempestuous tide,—
While land and waters each from each divide;
In concert sweet still rise our ardent prayer,
That each may be "the Lord's peculiar care."
Oh, shine on each, "Religion's tranquil ray,"
While in this darksome vale of life we stray;

Where joys and pains are closely intertwined,
And cares of earth corrode the Christian's mind.
Illume our path, thou ray of Love divine,
And on our mental darkness, sweetly shine;
Increase our fervour with increasing years,
Strengthen our faith, dispel our anxious fears;
Let Hope her anchor cast within the veil,
That fear of death may ne'er our souls assail.
Jesus, our pilot, calm the boisterous wave,
Our mortal part land in the peaceful grave;
When our frail barque on Canaan's shore shall rest,
May our rapt spirits dwell for ever with the Blest!

Mt. Parnassns. Con.

THE ORNAMENT OF WOMAN.

[WRITTEN IN AN ALBUM.]

Whose adorning,—let it be the hidden man of the heart, in that which is not corruptible, even the ornament of a meek and quiet spirit; which is in the sight of God of great price.—1 PET. iii. 3, 4.

THOUGH trite the themes, which fill the ALBUM's page,
Each well-intended offering we should prize;
For every scribbler cannot be a sage—
Yet truth is oftenest couched in homely guise.

Oft the didactick Muse her powers essays,
At the mild mandate of the female tongue,
To yield instruction in poetick lays,
Or chain the heart in melody of song.

And oft in poësy's seductive strains,
Sin's fatal toils entwine the female heart;
And while the foe's lethiferous power remains,
She strives in vain against the wiles of art.

Then how momentous, that her mind be stored
  With the wise precepts of the Gospel's page;
Which to her youth a safeguard, shall afford,—
  Bless her meridian, and support her age!

The mind, illumed by Science' genial light,
  And shielded with the panoply of grace,
Shall pass securely through the world's dark night,
  And prove victorious in her heavenly race.

How gracefully, upon the female brow,
  Blooms the bright wreath, Religion doth entwine!
And they, to Beauty or to Wealth, who bow,
  Will purer homage pay at *Virtue's* shrine.

Then let Religion's mild, benignant ray
  Shine in thy heart, and light Devotion's flame;
Illume thy path through life's eventful day,
  And crown thy exit with a *Christian's* fame.

Thus, shall thy soul aspire to realms above,
  To scenes of bliss, where pleasures never tire;
And in the embraces of IMMANUEL's love,
  Sound his immortal praise upon a Seraph's lyre!

ODE TO PEACE.

WRITTEN FOR THE FIRST ANNIVERSARY OF THE 'EAST HADDAM BRANCH OF THE MASSACHUSETTS PEACE SOCIETY;' DEC. 30, 1819.

[Tune, "Ode on Science."]

PHILANTHROPY! thou child of Light!
With robes of heavenly PEACE bedight;
How bleeds thy heart, when savage fight
    With slaughtered millions spreads the plain!
Hark! hear the din of arms resound!
Hear the shrill trumpet's warlike sound!
The neighing steeds—how fierce they bound,
    And prance o'er heaps of senseless slain!

Again the martial musick's swell
And victory's shout, too plainly tell,
That *Jubilee* is kept in hell,
    While men, like *demons*, men despoil.
For sure, a *fiendlike* rage alone
Can cause a brother's dying groan;
Then, fiends, while *kindred fiends* they own,
    'Grin horribly a ghastly smile!'

Shall this infernal, horrid train
For ever revel o'er the slain?—
Did Bethlehem's Star arise in vain?—
    Was *Peace* in vain announced on earth?—
—A ray of light beams from the skies;
The *Friend* of *Man* see WORCESTER rise,[4]
To wipe the tear from sorrow's eyes,
    And give to FELLOW-FEELING birth.

Come, heavenly PEACE! on balmy wing,
To thee we tune the vocal string;
Descend to earth, and with thee bring
    Release from misery and pain.
PHILANTHROPY! assert thy sway!
Let man no more his brother slay;
Oh, haste! thou blest MILLENNIAL Day!
    When UNIVERSAL PEACE shall reign

HOME.

"There's no place like Home."

[ON MY RETURNING FROM A TEMPORARY ABSENCE.]

HOME of my HEART! sweet REST from earthly care!
Once more I greet my dear domestick shrine;
Borne on affection's wing, I haste to share
In treasures, richer than *Potosi's* mine.

Home of my LOVE! though brief has been my stay,
Mid stranger-homes, and elemental strife;
How slowly seems to roll the car of day,
Estranged from children dear, and faithful wife.

Home of my JOY!—if joy abide not here,
'T is sought in vain throughout creation's range;
Here twine the tendrils of affection dear,—
A joy unknown to those who sigh for change.

Home of my HOPE! around this sacred hearth,
Are clustering buds of promise, fair and bright;
And what, *extraneous*, can to Hope give birth,
Like these dear objects, in the Father's sight!

Home of my PRAYER ! oh, let not sickness come,—
  No sad mischance, calamity, or death :—
Withhold my darlings from the insatiate tomb !—
  God of my fathers ! guard their vital breath !

Home of my FAITH ! yon glorious world above,
  There may we rest, when called to quit these scenes ;
For ever basking in a Saviour's love,
  To cloud whose rays no sorrow intervenes.

CHRISTIAN PHILANTHROPY.

INSCRIBED TO MY FRIEND J. F. MOORE, OF NEW YORK.

Let Avarice heap his hoards of glittering gold,
And grope his way in intellectual *night;*
Be mine the treasures wealth can ne'er unfold,
Disclosed to view through beams of mental light.

While peace and competence surround my board,
And bland affection cheers my labouring breast;
What further happiness can wealth afford,
Save, as a means to succour the distressed?

Yet something still, beyond the simple *means*,
Is requisite the sufferer's woes to heal;—
How rare the *miser's* breast to pity leans!
How rare, his callous heart hath power to feel!

But in proportion as his coffers shine,
His soul is veiled in penury's wretched pall;
Nor classick rays, nor holy truths combine,
To free his mind from *mammon's* lurid thrall!

What holier feelings sway the *Christian's* heart!
  Though fortune deigns not to increase his store,
'T is still his joy, with frugal means, to impart
  A needful pittance to the suffering poor.

Sweet sympathy asserts her heavenly power,
  Inspires his heart with pure affection's flame;
And fellow-man, relieved in misery's hour,
  Implores a benison on his loved name.

What then can earth detract from his pure joy,
  Though friends prove false, and wealth is torn away
His inward peace no outward ills annoy—
  He seeks his GUERDON *in the realms of day.*

LAUS SPIRITUI SANCTO.[5]

WRITTEN ON RECEIVING A LETTER FROM AN ABSENT DAUGHTER, ANNOUNCING THAT SHE HAD DEDICATED HERSELF TO HER SAVIOUR.

How welcome to the heart, when distant friends
Announce their welfare:—how the feeling breast
Dilates with joy, when fortune smiles serene,
And earthly prospects brighten to the view
Of those we love; when health's sweet voice is heard
Throughout their dwellings; when prosperity
Crowns all their labours, and felicity
Attends their earthly course, and sheds its beams
To cheer life's pilgrimage!

But if the heart,
With the report that temporal benefits
Attend our loved ones, is inspired with joy,—
How greater far, yea, how beyond the power
Of words to speak, shall heavenly transport rise
In the fond parents' heart, when news arrives
Their child is "born again!" Here bliss is found;

Bliss, sought in vain, and never known by those
Who seek their highest good in things of earth.
A joy is here, built on immortal base:
A child beloved is made an "heir of God,
Joint heir with Christ," inheritor of wealth—
A precious treasure—pearl of price unknown—
A pearl, a gem; with which, if once compared,
Earth's richest diadems are worthless dross.

And, oh! the wonders of redeeming Love!
How often sung, how oft extolled by man;
But, ah, how feeble man's best notes of praise!
Salvation, dearly purchased! yet how free!
Whence comes the treasure? Well may feeble man
Aghast with terror stand, if he but read
The dread behest, "work out your own salvation
With fear and trembling." Truly may he fear
And tremble, if the task devolve on him,
The creature of a day. But hope revives,
And courage nerves his heart, as on he reads
He has an help Almighty—"it is God
That worketh in you, both to *will* and *do*."
We own our help Almighty; and we feel—
Alas, our feeble nature feels and owns,
That, but for such an aid, our "work" were vain.

Then be the praise all THINE, Thou Mighty One!
"Not unto us, O Lord, not unto us,

But unto thy loved Name, be all the praise."
Praise to the Great Eternal! One in Three,
And Three in One, Thou *First* and *Last*, TRIUNE!
Thine be the hymn of praise, the ceaseless hymn
That swells its choral strain from every heart
Illumined by thy love; redeemed, set free,
Or yet on earth, or made a saint in Light.
And what employment so sublime as praise,
For the redeemed soul, while still detained
In fleshly pris'n, to suffer and to do
Her Maker's will?—what joy so ravishing;
What work, what labour, what employ so sweet?

And when the enraptured soul this "mortal coil
Hath shuffled off," and on triumphant wing,
Rich in the vestments of her Saviour's love,
Hath gained an entrance in the realms of rest,
Oh! how exhaustless is her theme of praise!
Praise to the Eternal Three, the great *I AM*—
The *Alpha* and *Omega*—GOD supreme:
To Christ, the Lamb, whose all-atoning blood,
On Calvary shed, redeemed a ruined world;
And to the Holy Ghost, "proceeding from
The Father and the Son," who holds third rank
In the Divine Hypostasis; whose breath,
Th' unseen *Afflatus*, irresistible,
Of power omnipotent, that, like the "wind

Blows where it listeth," penetrates the heart,
Controls the will, and brings the soul to God.

Spirit Divine! Thou source of light and joy!
Life of my life, and being of my soul!
Inspire a father's heart, that owns Thy sway,
That feels Thy power, and its own weakness feels;
O, let this heart its grateful tribute bring,
And laud that Mercy which hath saved my child!

The following poem is the pious effusion of a beloved daughter, to whom allusion was made in the preceding. It was first published in the New York Weekly Messenger, *and inscribed to her father; and it is here inserted on account of its immediate connection with the succeeding reply which it elicited.*

THERE'S NO PLACE LIKE HOME.

INSCRIBED TO N. L. F.

Yes, there 's *one* place like home, 't is at God's holy shrine,
Where high thoughts are kindled, and feelings divine;
Where the anthems of praise so melodiously roll,
There 's the home of devotion—the home of the *soul.*

As weary and sad, through this lone "vale of tears,"
Our steps we pursue, filled with doubts and with fears;
How the *Spirit's* sweet breathings calm peace can impart,
In this home of devotion—this home of the *heart!*

Though darkness and gloom overshadow our path,
And the world's blighting tempest comes on in its wrath;
Yet on Jesus' kind breast we repose all our care,
In this home of devotion—this sweet home of *prayer.*

As the Sabbath's calm hours we delightfully spend,
In holding high converse with Jesus, our friend;
Though often our thoughts to our absent friends roam,
Yet we feel that God's house is the christian's own home.

And trusting in Jesus, almighty to save,
We rob death of its sting—of its vict'ry, the grave;
All honour, and glory, and praise shall be given,
While we swell the full song, in that *better home—Heaven.*

Louisa.

New York, July 23, 1836.

TO LOUISA:—IN REPLY.

How dear to my heart is thy sweet aspiration,
At "God's holy shrine," so devoutly named "HOME;"
Where my daughter is wont in the way of salvation,
To withdraw from the world, and so joyfully come.

To this *home* once admitted, no labour nor sadness,
No doubts and no fears should oppress you with gloom;
But the "Spirit's sweet breathings" should fill you with gladness,
While welcomed a guest in the "christian's own home."

Oh! how sweet, at God's shrine, to pour forth adoration
To that Spirit divine, who hath caused your *new birth;*
Whose grace in your heart hath infused consolation,
And loosened the ties that once bound you to earth.

Greater joy, than to witness his child "in truth walking,"
Can the heart of your father on earth never bless;
And to hear his *Louisa* of JESUS' love talking,
Imparts a delight, which no words can express.

Then may my loved daughter find peace in believing,
And with patience advance in Christianity's race;
Avoiding sin's pathway—alluring—deceiving,
May she triumph victorious, a trophy of grace.

And when you have toiled through your day of probation,
And closed your devotions in God's earthly dome;
May your Saviour receive you, an heir of salvation,
And welcome your soul to the ***Christian's last home.***

Mt. Parnassus, Con., Aug. 3, 1836.

THE INVALID.

ARGUMENT.—*The value of Health—Its necessity to the enjoyment of life—Its uncertainty—The vanity of the world—Its transitory nature—The inefficiency of all earthly enjoyments to afford true Happiness—This is found only in Love to God, and true Religion; where the* INVALID *must look for comfort, and not to the world's sympathy—The certain termination of all terrestrial Joys—Prospect of Death—And Hope of Immortality.*

Sunt lachrymæ rerum, et mentem mortalia tangunt!—VIRGIL.

As when the weary traveller strives to gain
Some distant height, that overlooks the main;
And fondly hopes his weary limbs to rest,
Too long with labour and fatigue oppressed;
That summit gained, his disappointed eyes
See nought beyond, but plains that meet the skies;[6]
Desponding sinks; nor can ev'n hope impart
One ray to light the gloom which fills his heart!
—So *his* hard lot; whose being's only ray
Shines from the bourn of his terrestrial way;
Whose days of sickness and whose nights of pain
Form one unbroken, one continuous chain;

Whose frame no genial current ever warmed;
Whose ear health's grateful accents never charmed;
Who sees on earth no respite from his woe,
And looks in vain for happiness below;
Who finds no earthly treasures he may prize,
But hopes for rest alone in yonder skies.

The man, more favoured, ever blessed with health,
Knows not its value:—As the heir to wealth,
Inherited from his more prosperous sire,
Knows not the toil, which such acquests require.
Each found the treasure—and knows not to prize
The precious boon, which in his empire lies.

Devoid of ***Health***, what joy can earth afford,
Though ***Mammon*** smile, and ***Ceres*** crown the board?
Though fortune bless him with immense domains,
Can wealth relieve him of a moment's pains?
When on his cheek the livid hectick glows,
When anguish racks his frame with fiendlike throes,
And, like ***Prometheus***' vulture, rest denies,[7]
And dooms his days and nights to tears and sighs;
How vain, alas! the power of wealth to impart
A ray of comfort to his anguished heart!

Yet Health, this needful treasure, still we hold
By tenure as precarious as our gold:

Each may take wings, and disappoint our trust,
And lay our cherished prospects in the dust.
For, what on earth hath its foundation sure?
What laid so deep, that it can long endure?
Whate'er is *finite*, must to ruin tend;
For all that had beginning, must have end.
Who seeks, shall seek in vain, on earth to find
Joys, that alone should sate the immortal Mind.

See, on the stream of time, securely glide
The great—the gay—in all the pomp of pride.
The equipage of wealth, a gorgeous train,
Floats down the tide, and sails along the main.
In Fashion's gay parterre, see Beauty shine,
In all the splendour of Golconda's mine.
See Luxury preside o'er his domain,
Surrounded by his meretricious train.
See Pleasure revel in fantastick joys,
Where mere indulgence all true bliss destroys.
Pride apes imperial grandeur;—yet the more
His wishes prompt him to increase his store,
His better judgment must still more confess,
Though broader his domains, true joys are less.
Here bloated Indolence supinely rests,
And venal slaves obey his stern behests;
He spends his useless life in airy dreams,
And misery finds, in what enjoyment seems.

Such passing pageants strike the wondering gaze,
And call in question Heaven's all-righteous ways;
Till reason's ray pervades the Almighty's plan,
And vindicates the ways of Heaven to man:—
For nought shall counteract the all-wise decree—
Earth's highest glory is but vanity!

How evanescent Man's most brilliant state!—
The pomp and splendour of the proud—the great—
Recede from thought; and blank oblivion's pall
Shall shroud from view ev'n Man, the "lord of all:"
For Truth and Virtue only, shall survive,
And o'er the ruins of all nature live.

To yield true Happiness, alas, how vain
Are all earth's treasures—fruits of care and pain!
Unbounded wealth still leaves an aching void,—
As cares increase, is peace of mind destroyed;
And what, at distance viewed, we fancied joy,
When once possessed, proves but a useless toy.
—Is, then, felicity an idle dream,
Which floats o'er fancy, like a meteor gleam?
If sought in things of earth, the search is vain;
Earth's richest pleasures pay not half the pain;
And fancied bliss is oft but specious ill,
Fraught with no joys the heaven-born Mind should fill.

Ask we the path that leads to happiness?
Seek we those treasures, which alone can bless?

Oh, let our holy aspirations rise
To the great Fount of Good, above the skies.
The best affections of our hearts must soar
To the world's ARCHITECT, and God adore!
Religion's ray must pour its lucid beam,
To light our passage o'er Life's turbid stream.
In this, the *Invalid* may find that joy,
Which heartless selfishness cannot alloy.
How rare the gloom of his disastrous day,
Is cheered by Friendship's consolating ray!
To share his griefs, the worldling never deigns,—
No kindred feeling in whose bosom reigns;
For idol *self* absorbs the grovelling mind,
To others' ills and woes supremely blind:
And all the sympathy the SELFISH know
Is cold as *Zembla's* ever-during snow!

In youth's gay morn, how bright the prospect seems,
And cheats the fancy with delusive dreams.
We onward press, as Hope's sweet vision cheers,
Through the bright vista of increasing years;
And hope, through life, the pictured bliss to gain,—
Though disappointment proves each effort vain;
Till, at life's close, the truth must stand confessed
"Man never *is*, but always TO BE blessed."

Thus joys terrestrial, whether false or true,
Elude our grasp, and disappear from view.

What folly, then, to seek for good on earth,
Where only transitory joys have birth!
'T is reason's dictate, that we only prize
The bliss, that in RELIGION's empire lies.

For soon the brilliant scenes of life shall fade,
And our gay visions merge in Death's dark shade;
When all we fondly prized, and held most dear,
Will cease to charm, as we the tomb draw near.
Then, what we here possessed, or here enjoyed,
What pleased our fancy, or our senses cloyed,
Will nought avail:—then, *then* we learn to prize
The bliss, that in RELIGION's *empire lies!*

And then shall HE, whose being's brightest ray
Shines from the bourn of his terrestial way;
Whose days of sickness, and whose nights of pain,
Form one unbroken, one continuous chain;
Whose languid frame no genial current warmed,
Whose ear health's grateful accents never charmed;
Who sees on earth no respite from his woe,
And looks in vain for happiness below;
Who finds no earthly treasures he can prize,
Rejoice in hope of REST, in yonder glorious skies!

INTRODUCTION.

WRITTEN BY A FATHER IN HIS DAUGHTER'S ALBUM.[8]

My daughter asks her father to insert
A *Dedication* in her Album. Well,
Here he will write a father's best advice:
And when the heart which dictates, and the hand
Which writes it, shall be cold and motionless
In death's embrace—oh! may my daughter's heart
Receive instruction, as she casts her eye
O'er this instructive page. For, doubtless, oft
Her eye will scan these lines.

Then, call to mind
The image of your father, and the love—
The holy love—the ever-during flame,
That warmed his heart, when writing for his child!
Oh! call to mind his prayers—his anxious fears—
His deep solicitude—his cherished hopes—
His soul-warmed wishes—in his child's behalf!

And what his wishes are, full well you know.
Oft have you heard them uttered: Yet again

I here record—*I wish your* SOUL's *best good!*
And on this wish, I found my ardent hope,
That such may be the tenor of your life,
As to afford a parent's heart that joy—
That greatest of all joys—"to see his child
Walking in truth." *

Take, therefore, for your guide
God's holy volume; make that sacred Book
Your counsellor. Its precepts "read, mark, learn,
And inwardly digest," love, and obey.
Ask you for an exemplar?—Look to CHRIST!
In that bless'd Book his character is drawn;
His self-denying, painful life portrayed,
And still more painful death! Who reads, must love
His character,—his holy, spotless life.
And as you read the more, still more your love
Is drawn, in holy exercise, to rest
On this celestial Personage; this CHRIST,
The anointed One: this Saviour, JESUS; Lamb,
The Lamb of God; IMMANUEL, God with us.
Be this your pattern: follow where he leads:
His life—unsullied, pure, impeccable—
So far as imitable, imitate.
Devote yourself to him; and by his grace
Your death shall win the crown of endless life.

---

* 3 John, *ver.* 4.

Thus, to the MIND I dedicate your book;
To *mind*, heaven's noblest gift, distinctive trait
Of man; to *Virtue*, to *Religion*, *Sense*,
And *chastened sentiment*. Whate'er these claim,
What these require, what these approve,—insert.
But ne'er pervert this mental register,
Nor desecrate its page. No thought impure,
No sentence void of sense, no sentiment
Unworthy of the MIND, or which can raise
A blush upon the cheek of modesty,
Or give offence in aught, should enter here.
Be this your standard, then. For, those who read
Or hastily look o'er an Album's page,
Consider it, with strict propriety,
The approved index of its owner's mind.
Let yours, then, indicate a mind endowed
With richest lore; bright with Castalian dew;
Enriched with classick science; and illumed
With the pervasive rays of literature;
And—what is richer still, all price above—
Let pure religion, vital piety,
As a presiding genius, sit enthroned;
That her health-breathing spirit may appear,
As with a zone, to invest your mental stores,
To enhance their value, and to sanctify
All the acquirements gained by human art:—
For know, my daughter, that RELIGION'S ways
Are pleasantness, and all her paths are peace.

The following pathetick poem was written by this beloved daughter, and left in my cabinet, when she was going to reside abroad.

ADIEU.

ON LEAVING THE PATERNAL MANSION.

Father! now again I leave thee,
In the stranger's land to dwell;
Thou, who never didst deceive me,
Oh, receive this sad *Farewell!*

Mother! as thine eye is dwelling
On each child thou lov'st so well;
Think of her, whose heart is swelling,
As she breathes this fond *Farewell!*

Sisters! as soft eve is stealing,
Sing the hymn we loved so well;
And those tones, a grief revealing,
Will for me respond *Farewell!*

Brothers! whose young, sweet caressing,
On my heart has laid a spell;
Think, thy sister's heart-felt blessing
Mingles with this last *Farewell!*

Father! Mother! though we're parting,
And the tear-drops warm are starting;—
Sisters! Brothers! if no more
Meet we on this earthly shore;
May we all with Jesus dwell,
Never more to say Farewell!

Louisa.

TO MY DAUGHTER.

WRITTEN FOR HER BIRTH DAY; JANUARY 7.

Each year, in its flight, yields a theme for reflection;
Let this *Moralist*, then, your attention engage,
In youth's cheerful season, while yet no dejection
Shrouds life's brilliant morn in the darkness of age.

A thought of the future, in vision prospective,
Bright scenes of delight may unfold to the view;
Enchanting the thoughts, too, of years retrospective,—
The visions of youth picture joys in perspective,—
How often, alas! prove those visions untrue!

Louisa! give audience to reason's dictation,
O'er your mind let Religion maintain her mild sway;
Unshaken by skepticks' and fools' conversation,
In the strength of your Saviour, hold onward your way.

Should fortune prove faithless, and friends all forsake you,
Adversity barb her insidious dart;—
Faith, based on the sure Rock of Ages, will make you
On the Lord cast the sorrows that burden your heart.

So, when the last trump shall arouse all creation,
Triumphant to regions of bliss may you soar;
Each virtue, here loved, will endear your salvation,
Rich Grace claim your praises, while God you adore!

TO ELVIRA.

WRITTEN ON A SPLENDID SHEET OF PAPER, PRESENTED FOR THE PURPOSE.

THE Muse essays her loftiest powers,
Obedient to Elvira's call,—
To twine a wreath of richest flowers,
Though conscious, still, the boon is small.

Here, on this pure and stainless sheet,
The gift of *her* I hold so dear,
Would I inscribe an offering meet
For her, whose virtues I revere.

Cheered by mild friendship's genial ray,
Sustained by sympathy divine;
Fain would I tune my sweetest lay,
An offering at Affection's shrine.

For, in thy chaste and sinless breast,
An holy altar lights its fires;
Which no unhallowed thoughts molest—
Which no unchastened wish inspires.

And on that holy altar, burns
 Sweet incense, kindled with love's flame,—
Love, that this sentient heart returns,
 Nor seeks a meed of nobler fame.

My sister will accept this love;
 For, hearts, thus dearly intertwined,
Shall share in holier bliss above,
 In joys as lasting as the mind!

Our path through life is gemm'd with tears;—
 But, sister, there is bliss to come:
And hope in Christ dispels our fears,
 As we approach the lurid tomb.

For Jesus triumphed over death,
 And kindly here he guards his saints;
Supports us when we yield our breath,
 And pity gives to our complaints.

Here let us hold our onward course,
 That leads to deathless joys on high;
Where we shall praise of Love the Source,
 And live, and love,—no more to die.

And there, in sweet seraphick strains,
 We'll join the choir around the Throne,
Who praise, throughout the heavenly plains,
 Day without night, the THREE IN ONE!

TO ELVIRA.

WRITTEN FOR HER BIRTH-DAY; JUNE 4.

LET thy loved brother, on thy *natal day*,
Attune his lyre, and chant a modest lay
To his *Elvira*:—sweetly flow the strain,
That for a while may ease thy heart of pain.

O, that the auspicious day, which saw thy birth,
Might, with each revolution of the earth,
Witness contentment sparkling in thine eyes,—
Nor thy loved bosom heaved with painful sighs!

But ah! how sure is grief our nature's doom,
Till we descend into the peaceful tomb!
In this decree, how sad has been thy part,—
And Grace, alone, can heal thy bleeding heart!

Beloved sister! in thy griefs I share,
Respond thy sighs—participate thy care;
In all thy nameless ills I sympathize
And wipe the tears that glitter in thine eyes.

And wipe the tears?—alas, the attempt were vain!—
Then let mine flow, in sympathetick pain,—
Mingle my griefs with thine;—for sure my heart
In others' woes can bear a feeling part.

And oh! there's joy in grief! Who would resign
This precious treasure, for earth's richest mine?
In souls congenial, joys and sorrows blend,
And indicate the generous, sterling FRIEND.

What words shall paint the emotions of my soul,
Who yields her powers to love's benign control;—
That chastened flame, which warms the pious breas
And antedates our bliss, in realms of heavenly rest!

TO MISS L. F. M——, OF NEW YORK.

ON THE ANNIVERSARY OF HER BIRTH: MARCH 12.

LIGHT breaks from the east, the bright landscape disclosing
 Yon glorious orb rises full on the sight;
Day dawns o'er the scene, late in darkness reposing,
 Illuming creation—dispersing the night.
A type thus presenting, of that holy morning,
 From darkness and death, when the world shall arise;
Our dust called to life, and our souls grace adorning,
 Secure we shall soar to yon orient skies.

Time rapidly glides! and when past its rotation,
 Eternity's era unceasing shall run;
Restored to new being, the heirs of salvation,
 May we shout *Hallelujah*, for victory won!
Oh, then, while we sojourn in this fleshly prison,
 Our hopes let us rest on *Immanuel's* Love;
Rejoicing in faith—that, as JESUS has risen,
 Earth cannot detain us from mansions above.

9

TOKEN OF ESTEEM.

INSCRIBED TO W. E. M——, OF NEW YORK.

(Written at parting.)

Why labours the breast with this gush of warm feeling—
  Humanity's tide bursting forth from the eye?—
Intense is the anguish, that, o'er the heart stealing,
  Transforms our delight into misery's sigh!

Bland sympathy pours her spontaneous effusion,
  Yielding transient delight, yet commingled with pain;
Each vision of bliss is replete with delusion,
  Most prone to extend Disappointment's domain.

Entranced with the prospect, in youth how alluring;
  Repulsive and odious, possession may prove;
Sad experience evinces, that nothing enduring
    On earth can be found, that is worthy our love.

No longer, my friend, let this world's fleeting treasure
  Mock your sight, and transfix you with misery's dart;
Oh, how poignant the knowledge, that what we call *pleasure*,
  Oft mingles enjoyment with sorrow's keen smart!—
Religion's delights can alone fill the measure,
  Eternally yielding pure Joy to the heart.

Aug. 11, 1836.

A TRIBUTE OF AFFECTION.

TO MISS A. E. M——, AT PARTING.

THE truth again obtrudes—that painful truth,
Which, erst, ELVIRA read in my dull lays—
'How impotent are *words* to speak the *heart!*'
Yet still a strange delight comes o'er each sense,
While, with these *feeble indices of mind*,
I trace the heart's emotion!

Here I come—
I meet your warm embrace: your feeling heart
Responds to mine—a heart of kindred warmth:
The tearful eye beholds its image in
An eye as tearful: soul with soul unites.
A rapture thrills each breast, and paints the joys
Of heaven; while on the scene of this communion,
The delegated spirit of the Highest
May deign the unblushing, the approving smile!
No sordid views, no sinful thoughts intrude,
To blight this holy feeling! Each for each
Prefers a prayer, *that Heaven, to each, be kind!*

Perhaps, who chance to read the poet's strain,
May claim an outline of his history.

Know then, though sorrow is the lot of man,
That "sorrow, like my sorrow," few have known.
The last surviver of my father's house—
Not much unlike the "scathed pine," I stand
A beacon to the world—a living proof
That sorrow, anguish, care, bereavement, death,
Are foreordained man's cheerless heritage!

In the cold bosom of our kindred earth,
Our common *alma mater*, in the soil
Of *three* New England states,—repose the *manes*
Of my progenitors—the progeny
Of STANDISH—pilgrim father—puritan—
Foremost among the *hundred* pious ones,
Who, 'mid December's icy blasts, debarked
On PLYMOUTH'S *bleak, inhospitable shore,*
Where, dashed on rocks, the broken billows roar!
There, too, my kindred, in collateral line,
All—ALL repose! for Death not one hath spared,—
Death, sateless tyrant! And the grave, insatiate,
Found want of room in all New England's soil!
For, this magnanimous, imperial state
Holds, in her wide domain, my kindred dust.
Near Brooklyn's heights, unhonoured with a stone
To point Affection to his lowly bed,
Repose the ashes of God's minister,
The reverend EMERSON.

But thee, *lorn fair one!*
The tender branch of that beloved stock,

By chance I found surviving; and I come
To greet thee, loved one! on this distant shore.
With 'holy kiss' I greet thee—that same kiss,
With which St. Paul once told us each to greet.
And now, like him, "I go, bound in the spirit,"
Of "things which shall befall me," ignorant;
Yet fully prescient, that "bonds and afflictions
Abide me" still: But, by the grace of God,
"None of these things doth move me; nor count I
My life dear to myself, if but I may
Finish my course with joy; and well perform
The work my Lord hath trusted to my hands."

Well—now, the greeting o'er, the time elapsed
I bid adieu!—I mount the fragile barque
That waits to waft me from thy loved embrace!
Elvira! weep not; though I still pursue
Paul's glowing strain—"Ye see my face no more."
Yet, this I say not—hope it be not so:
God grant we meet again on this side heaven.
—All earthly happiness hath this alloy—
The day of parting comes: the trying hour
Of separation surely will arrive.

I leave you here with your few precious friends:
I go to my loved home—yon "rugged realms"—
My favourite "Parnassus;" there to join[9]
"My soul's far dearer part," wife of my youth,
And share again the joys of home—'sweet home.'
Thence, through my favourite medium, 'ink and pen,'

Oft will I greet *Elvira:* and, perchance,
This valued "Messenger and Advocate"
Will sometimes be the vehicle, which bears
The votive reminiscence of thy friend.

Then, once again, *Adieu!* though hard the word
Of utterance,—though my feeble frame almost
Denies me strength to wend my way from you,—
Although my stricken heart can scarce resist
This harsh vibration of its finest strings;—
Still I must say, Adieu!

Long—long shall I
Remember this dear interview, this *home*—
The kindness here received,—this cordial greeting;
The anxious care, the deep solicitude,
To minister to the necessities
Of this sick, feeble body,—weak and frail,
And soon to be dissolved.

All I can give—
My thanks, my love, my prayers—I freely give.
In heaven we part not. Here we wait God's will:
Regard not time,—or long, or short; if when
The summons comes, our lamps be trimmed, and we
Found duly watching. Then aloft we soar,
To realms of peace, where death can part no more;
Where, whatsoever bliss the soul employ,
The thought that 't is eternal, crowns the joy!

New York, Oct. 13, 1834.

DIRGE.

COMMEMORATIVE OF MISS AMELIA S. CHAPMAN, OF EAST HADDAM.

Respectfully inscribed to her bereaved Parents.

How oft have I the mournful Muse invoked,
To paint the scenes, where, with a ruthless step,
Relentless Death hath trod the floweret down.
And, Oh! how thick such scenes come clustering round!
One grave is scarcely closed, ere we behold
Another, and another, opening wide
To seize the richest, dearest joys of earth,
And in its sateless womb, from human view
For ever to enshroud them!—Here, we mourn:
Friends die! hearts bleed!—the heritage of earth.
Why, else, had not AMELIA been immortal?
Joy of her parents' heart; hope of their age;
Embellished with acquirements rich and rare;
Enrobed with piety, with grace endued;—
Too soon, alas! she 's summoned to the skies.
How strange, how unexpected fell the shaft!

Noiseless and secret as the pestilence
That walks in darkness, came the messenger,
The fell disease, that minister of death,[10]
Whose sway too oft the healing art defies,
And cities, towns, and villages despoils!
But here destruction's besom seemed to *spare*,
For "*one* is taken, and the other left." [11]
The loveliest floweret is the soonest plucked,
As thieves will first the ripest fruit invade.

Too selfish mortals, we would here detain
A sister spirit from her native skies—
A spirit ripe for immortality.
We want her dear society, her love—
Her bright example longer here to shine,
To add acumen to the parting scene!
For parting scenes must come. And, O! how blest—
How blest the one, who first is summoned hence:—
For nature feels and owns the painful truth
'When such friends part, 't is the surviver dies!'

Ye weeping parents, brothers, sister, friends—
And I among her *friends* must claim a rank—
My *pupil* once—I mourn her early doom—
Ye mourn not without hope: joy fills your hearts,
Joy rises midst your grief, that she was spared
To be the subject of a *second birth*;
That Jesus' love had found her, and his grace

Made her a trophy of his blood-stained cross.
This thought alone can cicatrize the wound
Of bleeding sensibility. Yet still
Affection lingers round *Amelia's* grave,
And drops the tear humanity must shed,
As all her lovely charms pass in review:
Her mild deportment and her modest mien,
Her winning manners and her cultured mind,
The amiable graces of a heart
Alive with fellow feeling, and replete
With sensibility and christian love.
'Tis thus is felt the value of that gem
Her weeping friends have lost. But, this our loss
Is her eternal gain. Then let her grave
Speak forth instruction, and a lecture read
To her surviving friends. Earth and her charms,
Her fascinating charms, are all beneath
The aspirations of the immortal *mind.*

To higher joys and nobler wealth aspire,
And let religion's flame your bosom fire;
Seek ye an interest in a Saviour's love,
To fit your souls for endless bliss above;
That, with this blest inheritance in view,
You may with joy bid scenes of earth adieu.

THE LIGHT OF SCIENCE AND REVELATION.

How bright, athwart life's darksome way,
Fair Science darts her lucid ray,
To bless us with its sheen!
Her magick power unbarred the prison—
O'er nature's darkness light has risen
To cheer the sombre scene.

And, but for this pervasive ray,
Sepulchral night were still our day,
And ignorance our doom:
Omniscient Providence designed
A RESURRECTION for the MIND,
From such a mental tomb!

Free from the thrall of adverse powers,
A goodly heritage is ours—
On us sweet science shines:
Here *Mind* asserts her birth-right dower,
Redeemed from Superstition's power,
And opes exhaustless mines!

Here she pursues her upward way,
And fearless tracks the realms of day,
To scan the stellar zone;

With philosophick ken she finds
Worlds, that circumfluent ether binds,
    And calls them all her own.

The wonders of the mighty deep
She calls from their long night of sleep,
    And ushers into day;
Whate'er the solid spheres contain,
What cuts the air, or skims the plain,
    Is subject to her sway.

The FEMALE MIND, too long oppressed
By barbarous ignorance,—now redressed,
    Asserts her native right:
Now female genius well may claim
Her station on the ROLL of FAME,
    In lineaments of light!

Yet, all this light were lost in gloom,
Beyond the confines of the tomb,
    Had not the Omnifick Will
Shed on the mind the Gospel's ray,
To light us with perennial day,
    To Zion's holy hill.

Then while these precious gifts we prize,
Let incense from our hearts arise,
    To Him who gave them all:—
For that best gift, GOD's only Son,
While everlasting ages run,
    Prostrate in praise we'll fall.

THE DYING MOTHER.

A FRAGMENT.

The summons comes! the harbinger of grief,
That calls us to the bed, whereon reclines
Our last surviving parent!—I have mourned
The loss of *all my kindred*:—Ye have heard—
For oft the mournful story I have told—
That, of my father's house, *I sole survive:*
And still bereavement comes; for here, alas!
I'm *wedded* to affliction. On this couch,
And just within Death's grasp, a mother lies—
The mother of my SPOUSE, my *second self.*

Though I could wish I had been spared the sight,
Yet not the pious hand of filial love
Shall here be wanting, or in aught remiss,
To close her dying eyes; while life remains
To list her accents, or to pour the voice,
At her desire, of fervent prayer to Heaven.

Oh, see! a *mother's love*, how strong in death!
She speaks—extends her feeble, nerveless hands—
She clings to life: for yet, even yet, her heart,
The native home of pure maternal love,
The seat of every holy sympathy,
Of bland philanthropy—pure love to man—
That feeling heart still holds in its embrace
Her weeping children; haply present, all,

To minister to her necessities;
To smooth—so far as filial piety,
Innate, and cherished in most feeling hearts,
Has power to "smooth—the rugged pass to death."

Yes, that mild eye still beams a mother's love:—
She would stay longer with us, here to share
Awhile our joy or sorrow—weal or woe;
Still she would bless us with a mother's love—
A mother's presence; and continue still
To impart those pious counsels, which so long
Have been a *Pharos* to our darkling way.
She would recover strength, ere she goes hence;
For, oh! how dearly she her children loved!
She still would clasp them in her widowed arms,
And even awhile the promised bliss forego,
Which waits her advent in the realms of rest,
That here a little longer she might stay
To bless her *fatherless* and weeping ones.
"A mother's fondness cannot be conceived
But by a mother." Is there here on earth,
A love more stainless, ardent, and sincere?
—But the keen pains which rack her feeble frame
Premonish her that she must soon depart.
And though this life has charms and mystick ties
That bind her still to earth, and seem to check
The heaven-aspiring spirit; yet she bows
To Heaven's just mandate, and submissive cries—
"My Father calls; and let His will be done!"

* * * * * *

The soul has fled! No more the fleshly prison
Retards the flight of its ethereal guest.
Spirit ethereal—viewless—breath of God!
Whither, oh! whither gone? The spirit-land,
That undiscovered realm whence none return,
Where, *where* is its locality!—Unknown,
Unseen by mortal vision; unconceived;
Yet held within the ken of Nature's God,
The world's great Architect! Sufficient, this,
For darkling man to know, that all is right;
That all is safe in an Almighty hand:
That each constituent part, Matter and Mind,
Shall in due time appear; and purged from dross,
If in the SAVIOUR found, be clothed in white
And put on immortality,—the robe
By JESUS purchased.
Then, why need we weep,—
Though *orphans* named on earth?—Our stay is short;
The counsels of our mother still abide
Engraven on our hearts; and her example
Exists in memory's vision, and entreats
Our faithful emulation; and though now
We have in heaven more friends than here on earth,
We'll patient wait all our appointed time,
And bow submissive to the will of Him,
Whose gracious promise is—*" Thine orphans leave;
Them I will keep, and will preserve alive."

Feb. 1835.

---

* Jer. xlix. 11.

DITHYRAMBICK: TO LOUISA.

NUPTIAL ANNIVERSARY, MAY 30.

AGAIN, ye tuneful NINE! I ask your aid,
To inspire my soul with pure seraphick fire;
LOUISA claims my lay:—to her were paid
My vows in youth:—once more my soul inspire.

Oft have ye deigned your aid;
Your votary, oft I 've prayed,
And called you all by name:
When, erst, in ardent youth,
And since, in manhood's truth,
I 've hymn'd *Louisa's* peerless fame.

URANIA, muse divine! my thoughts inspire,
And lovely CLIO, lend your wonted fire;
CALLIOPE,
MELPOMENE,
And POLYHYMNIA, join the tuneful choir:
And TERPSICHORE, gay,
And comick THALIA,
ERATO, priestess at young Cupid's fane,
And sweet EUTERPE, swell the choral strain!

Whatever names ye bear,
Whatever titles wear,

Whatever office is to each assigned;
From realms of light descend,
Your inspiration lend,
Breathe into *matter* your ethereal *mind*.

But why implore the Muses' aid,
When I *Louisa's* praises sing?
Spirit of LOVE! celestial Maid!
Come, and thy annual offering bring.

Celestial Dove,
Immortal Love!
Thy sacred influence impart;
While I again,
In votive strain,
Breathe the free offering of my heart.

Nineteen short years their circling course have run,
Since first I called *Louisa* mine;
My plighted faith, with each returning sun,
Has decked the Hymeneal shrine.

As erst I sung, in strains to thee,
Louisa, on this Jubilee,
'Record with me the genial lay,
How sweet is Love's perennial sway.'

From God each gift descends;
To God our thanks be paid;
Though He our best and dearest friends
Low in the dust hath laid;

Yet still his goodness crowns our fleeting days,—
Be ours, to render glad returns of praise.

Come, then, with me ascend on ardent wing,
And soar beyond the realms of stellar light;
Of Love divine, of boundless Wisdom sing,
Nor grope in darkness, and in mental night.

To God, who crowns our joy,
Let grateful anthems rise;
His praise our loftiest notes employ
Who plann'd the earth and skies.

While Justice frowns, and blights our schemes,
And dissipates our brightest dreams;
His Mercy shines,
In fairest lines,
And *good* is meant, where *evil* seems.

Then let us on his grace rely,—
No murmurs e'er perturb our breast;
His bounty shall our wants supply,
And yield us calm and heavenly rest.

Ye Nine! adieu;
What more can you,
Than light your poet's humble fire?
The poet's bays,
Louisa's praise,
Is all the meed, to which my views aspire.

THE DAY OF REST.

And God rested on the seventh day from all his work. GEN. II. 2.

The Angel said unto them, Why seek ye the living among the dead? He is not here, but is risen. ST. LUKE, XXIV. 5, 6.

HAIL! holy SABBATH morn
How welcome to the soul, thy quiet rest!
Prelusive to the calm which waits the Blest,
When deathless life is born.—
—Hail! holy Sabbath morn!

This day the SAVIOUR rose!
No bars of death could hold him in the tomb;
The rising God emerged in beauty's bloom:—
In vain the guards oppose—
The Almighty Saviour rose!

How tranquil is this dawn!
All nature, hushed in heavenly quiet, lies;
Rekindling light illumes the eastern skies,
And over hill and lawn,
Lights up this tranquil dawn.

Let man arise, and praise!
With vocal Nature join his votive breath;—
In praise of him, who triumphed over death,
Let every creature raise
The hymn of grateful praise!

And did our JESUS die?—
What matchless love his holy bosom fired!
The Son of God—the Friend of man—expired,
And in the grave did lie:—
For *man* did JESUS die!

For man the Saviour rose!
He captive led captivity—above—
Into his Father's courts, the realms of Love,
Where pleasure's fountain flows;
And triumphed o'er his foes.

Praise to the Saviour, give!
In concert join, all beings, great and small,
And hymn the praises of the Lord of all:
To Him, by whom ye live,
Praise to IMMANUEL, give!

Hail! holy *Sabbath* morn!
How grateful to the soul, thy placid REST!
A Sabbath, without end, awaits the Blest;
For deathless LIFE was born,
On this refulgent morn!

MEDITATIONS AT MIDNIGHT.

[ON THE COUCH OF SICKNESS.]

'Tis midnight's fearful hour!—Around me flit
Aerial spirits, watchmen of my sleep—
Or, rather, of my *vigils:* For, alas!
"Sleep, like the world, his ready visits pays
Where fortune smiles: the wretched he forsakes;
Swift on his downy pinions flies from woe,
And lights on lids unsullied with a tear."
No marvel, then, he flies this lowly couch;
For here he finds not fortune's favourite;
And, sure, if tears repel his kind approach,
'T is marvellous, indeed, I ever sleep!

Exhausted nature woos his soothing power,
And craves his renovating influence.
Yet I lament not his capriciousness,
Nor mourn his coyness: while I thus enjoy

These soul-inspiring vigils, fraught with love;
Presenting heavenly views; engendering thoughts
That raise the MIND superior to the rack
Of corporal anguish, and absorb those pains,
Whose piercing darts pervade the mortal frame;
With perspiration drench it; circumvest
The heart—the breast—each macerated limb;
Accelerate the feverish pulse; and round
The throbbing temples place a deadening weight.
—I *wake* for LORE: and vigils teach the mind,
If on th' attainment of true science bent.
The MIND, that made and governs all, ne'er sleeps!
For, this fair fabrick of creation, else,
Without his constant and directing rule,
Would to primeval chaos soon return.
Yes; though thick darkness mantles o'er the world,
And all creation in profound repose
Unconscious lies; creation's Architect
Ne'er quits the helm, nor once unmindful proves
Of the unnumbered, multifarious wants
Of all the creatures of his plastick hand!

Consoling thought!—and does he think of *me*,
A feeble, sick, dependant, dying worm?
Yes—blessed be his name! He cares for ALL.
For, "not a sparrow falleth to the ground
Without our heavenly Father:" and we have
The kind assurance, that "of value more

Than many sparrows," in our Father's mind
We are esteemed. His providential care
Pervades all nature: and this care to prove
How manifold—abundant—passing rich—
He "gives his angels charge concerning us."
Celestial spirits swim the liquid air,
At midnight, and encamp around my couch.
Cherubick visitants! beloved, unseen;
Present, though viewless! The sweet consciousness,
That ye surround my path, asleep—awake—
That, agents of the ETERNAL, ye are sent
On messages of love,—to keep me safe
From "pestilence that in the darkness walks,"—
From the "destruction that at noon-day wastes,"—
Brings consolation to my labouring breast.

Would the divine economy permit,
How would I hold sweet intercourse with you!
O, were the spirit-language known to me,
With rapt delight my spirit would ascend
And mingle with you; dear communion hold,
And learn your Order, in high Heaven's ranks;—
Seraph, or Cherub, Thrones—Dominions—Powers—
Souls of the JUST, made perfect!—or, perchance,
The disembodied MINDS of long-lost Friends!

O! thought enrapturing! Is my *Father* near?
My Mother—Sisters—Brother, ever dear?

Oh, for some recognition!—I would see,
And recognise, a soul, from flesh set free!
Yet, Heaven forefend, that, with presumption, I
Should in the mysteries of the ETERNAL pry!
Submissive to his will, O let me wait,
Nor ask the secrets of the future state;
Last of my House, though I remain alone,
And on the bed of sickness pine and groan;
Indulgent God! forbid one anxious sigh,
Though tears of fond remembrance dim my eye!
Let tears of deep contrition copious roll,
And heartfelt penitence subdue my soul;
And though I weep my numerous kindred, dead,
May tears of gratitude be also shed:—
Endeared by holiest tie, SHE still remains,
The "gift of God," sweet soother of my pains.
When pain and anguish on our state attend,
How doubly dear, a sympathizing friend!
How the *kind offices*, in sickness, bind
Our grateful hearts to a *congenial mind!*
They only, who enjoy, can know to prize
The holy boon, that in affection lies!

While swells my heart with gratitude to Heaven,
For all the *earthly good* which God has given;
For *heavenly gifts*, more grateful notes should rise,
And swell the tide of praise in upper skies!

For that blest Gospel, whose mysterious light
Pervades the darkness of sepulchral night;
For that rich gift, the SAVIOUR's precious blood,
Which purged our sins, and ransomed us to God;
For all the means of grace, with which we 're blest,
Which gives an earnest of immortal rest;
For that blest Faith, which cheers our earthly way,
And pours o'er death's dark vale a guiding ray;—
For Hope, through CHRIST, of rising from the tomb,
In his dear image—clad in youthful bloom—
Convoyed by angels to the *Saviour's* breast,
To spend eternity amidst the Blest;—
O, may my heart with pure affection glow,
Nor carnal wish, nor selfish motive know;
But ceaseless Gratitude my soul inspire,
And train my thoughts to Heaven's all-bounteous Sire:
May bland Religion's sanctified control
Prune every wish, and purify my soul;
And let my lips, on earth, commence the lay,
Which, ceaseless, swells, in realms of endless day!

July 10, 1838.

THOUGHTS PENNED IN A SICK ROOM.

INSCRIBED TO MY DAUGHTER.

'T is greatly wise to talk with our past hours,
And ask them, what report they bore to Heaven;
And how they might have borne more welcome news.
DR. YOUNG.

ETERNAL WISDOM ne'er designed
This world should be our resting place;
For, sure, the imperishable *Mind*,—
When we have run our earthly race
And closed this scene of mortal strife,—
Will *just have entered into life!*

The *rudiments of being*, then,
This life, appropriately, we name;
Though far beyond our reason's ken,
The END, for which we hither came,
To inhabit this terrestrial sphere,
And pass a short probation here.

The utmost stretch of human sight,
Although too limited to see,—
JEHOVAH's plans can but be right;
Our reason bows, O Lord! to Thee!

In Thy blest Volume let us look,
And make our guide Thy Holy Book.

As we its sacred pages scan,
  We find, for what we 're stationed here;
They tell us—the chief end of man
  Is, God to love, obey, and fear;
That deathless life we may employ
Our God for ever to enjoy.

When pain and sickness rack the frame,
  And teach—*how frail is human life;*
Oh, let them wake Religion's flame,
  Call home our thoughts, repress our strife:
Then, with past hours how wise to talk,
That, heaven-ward, we in peace may walk!

Sickness and trials, care and pain,
  Are kindly sent, our Faith to test;
They teach us, Earth's supports are vain,
  And point to Heaven's enduring rest:—
That all our strength is from above,
That all our hope—the Saviour's love.

'T is wisdom, to review the past,
  And hold communion with our heart;
O'er former years our thoughts to cast,
  Resolved to act a wiser part;—
The errors of past years to mend,
And seek, in Jesus Christ, a *Friend.*

"A bed of death detects the heart"—
  A *sick-bed,* too, is rich in lore;
Reflection oft may truth impart—
  The spirit's breathings light will pour
O'er Death's dark vale, as we draw nigh
That PORTAL *to* THE UPPER SKY!

Then, oft, my Daughter, think of Death,
  And keep Eternity in sight;
So, when thou shalt resign thy breath,
  In *that drear pass,* a cheering light
Will point thee where thy SAVIOUR lay,
Who is "the Life, the Truth, the Way."

TO LOUISA.

FROM HER FRIEND, WHILE FAR AWAY.

O, HOW do my thoughts cluster round thy dear dwelling,
  The HOME, where this heart hath so long found its rest!
O, how doth this bosom, with sympathy swelling,
  Most ardently pant, with thine own to be pressed.

As o'er the broad waste, that creates separation
  From all the loved treasures my heart holds most dear,
With longing I gaze, and devout contemplation,—
  How my vision is dimmed with the unbidden tear!

No kindness from strangers, affection revealing,
  Compensates the loss which this bosom sustains;
With attentions caressed, I am vainly concealing
  The anguish my heart so incessantly pains!

Around thy loved fireside, the voice of affection
  Is heard, in such strains as would gladden my heart;
Estranged from that fireside, no earthly connection
  Has power to delight,—or can pleasure impart.

Like the Dove from the Ark, borne on tremulous pinion,
I scan the dark waters, and long to return ;
The endearments of home still assert their dominion,
And connubial affection unceasing shall burn.

Yet, to thy behest, O thou God of salvation !
I bow in submission ;—and on THEE would cast
My cares and my burdens—in sweet resignation,
Assured, " to thy lambs thou wilt temper the blast."

My journeyings o'er, and the waters subsided,
Restore me again to the home of my heart ;
Preserved by thy grace—by thy Providence guided—
Oh, let me return—never more to depart.

To thy will in submission, the race set before us
May we patiently run, and contend for the prize ;
And, oh, may thy guidance for ever be o'er us,
And conduct us to rest, in yon glorious skies.

There safely arrived,—and our pilgrimage ended,—
Uniting in praise, with the ransomed above ;
Our notes, with seraphical symphonies blended,
Shall swell the rich chorus to JESUS'S LOVE !

Baltimore, Dec. 25, 1838.

THE SABBATH.

Hold fast the form of sound words.—2 Tim. i. 13.

I love the holy Sabbath! O, how sweet,
How welcome, is this sacred day of rest!
And how delightful, wheresoe'er I go,
To join the worship of my own dear Church!

In duty's path, I wander from my home—
From my domestick shrine—from the embrace
Of my loved family; and pass my days,
My many tedious days, and weeks, and months,
'Mid stranger-homes, in feeble health—*alone!*
But, ever, joyous is this day's return.
I love the holy Sabbath! day of Rest!
Rest from my toils, my daily, wearying toils.
For body and for mind, here is repose.
—I enter Zion's courts, the house of God;
And here, throughout Columbia's happy land
Of civil and religious liberty,
I find the Church. With joy I enter in,
And take a part in her delightful "Form
Of words most sound," devout and rational;
And think—how many thousand thousand more
Throughout the christian world, are then engaged
In use of that incomp'rable Liturgy,

Which saints, apostles, martyrs long have made
A medium of communion with their God:—
And while I think, the very thought gives joy,
That thousand thousand voices now are tuned
To pour their simultaneous praises forth
To God, in this same sapient "Form of words."
Thus, distant friends in sweet communion meet,
Though seas and land divide—from pole to pole;
Though earth's diameter be interposed;
Though rolls the Atlantick or Pacifick wave
To sunder friend from friend; whose hearts, perchance,
In pondering o'er the distance, may be pained;
Yet, in this holy service when engaged,
And offering prayers to heaven, in these "same words,"
They sweet communion hold, and seem to feel
And recognise a dear proximity,
As thus their prayers in unison ascend
An offering pure, an holy sacrifice.

Oh! in such scenes, how often has my heart
Embraced my dear, my absent family,
Whom I supposed engaged in praising God
In the same Church *on earth*—in these "same words!"
How sweet the tie, that binds in christian love
The hearts of Christians! And how sweet to pour
Our voice in notes symphonious; where no jar,
No discord mars the strains; but voice with voice
In concord sweet resounds; and soul with soul

In dear communion mingles, while the voice
Of each to each responsive, in its turn,
Conspires to swell the tide of sacred praise
To the all-bounteous, omnipresent GOD!

I love the SABBATH! May I ever love,
And with increasing fervour, more and more
Love, cherish, honour, sanctify and keep,
As God commands, His holy Sabbath day!
And when this feeble tenement, which seems
Consuming slowly, but by progress sure,
Shall be dissolved, peaceful may I repose
In kindred dust, and sweetly sleep in CHRIST!
Then, with renascent frame, building of God,—
"An house not made with hands," assimilate
Unto the glorious body of my Lord,—
May I arise, purged from all earthly dross,
And fresh with life, a trophy of the Cross,
In mid air meet my Lord; and, saved by grace,
In Heaven's bright mansions find an humble place;
Where, having prized on earth the Sabbath's rest,
I hail an endless SABBATH with the BLEST.

LOVE PURE AND ARDENT;
FAITH, UNSHAKEN;
SORROW AND GRIEF, INTENSE AND HEART-WITHERING;
JOY, UNPARALLELED AND INEFFABLE:
AS EXEMPLIFIED IN

MARY.

ST. JOHN, XX. 1—16.

THROUGHOUT the SAVIOUR'S residence on earth;
What a conspicuous place does WOMAN hold!
What matchless Love is shown—what steadfast Faith;
What humble, yet what friendly offices—
The dictates of affection—were performed!

The contents of the alabaster-box*
Of precious ointment, though of cost immense,
Which on the Saviour's sacred head were poured,
Rank less in value, than those precious tears
That laved his feet. These spoke the ardent love
Of her, whose "sins were many;"† and this love,
Which led her to her Lord, to wash his feet
With flowing tears, and wipe them with her hair,

* Mark, xiv. 3. Luke, vii. 37, *et seq.* † Luke, vii. 47.

And on them to imprint affection's kiss,—
Evinced such FAITH, such heart-felt penitence,
That He, "to whom all hearts are open," said,
"Her sins are pardoned; for she loved much."

Nor ever waned that love. For, at the Cross
Stood this same MARY, and the other *two*,
The Virgin-Mother, and Cleophas' wife.*
Yes,—by the Cross they stood, on that sad day,
That memorable "preparation day,"
On which transpired the sanguinary scene—
The scene which our Salvation's drama closed!
This scene they witnessed: and the dying words,
The solemn "IT IS FINISHED!" met their ears;
Nor left the funeral train, till they beheld
The sepulchre, and how his corpse was laid.†
And though they home returned, yet were their hearts
Within his tomb: their faithful love prepared
Ointments and spices to embalm their Lord,‡
Ere they could seek the Sabbath's tranquil rest.

That Sabbath past, "the first day of the week,
While yet 't was dark," came MAGDALENE forth[12]
Unto the sepulchre. Grief filled her heart.
Ruled by commandment of the Jewish law,

---

* John, xix. 25. † Luke, xxiii. 55. ‡ Luke, xxiii. 56.

The sabbath-day she rested.* But her love
Prevents the dawn, and leads her to the tomb
To view the body of her murdered Lord,
And pour her soul in sorrow! For as yet
The scripture was not fully understood,
That CHRIST, the first-born of the tomb, should RISE.
Hers was that settled grief, that blank despair,
Which bids defiance to the graphick powers,
And beggars ev'n conception. Such a grief
As *hers*, can now be neither felt, nor feared.
She mourned her dearest Friend *for ever* lost:—
For, then, no tenant of the tomb had risen;
Renascent life had never burst death's bars;
She wept—she mourned—she grieved, as without hope!
Her love still lingered round his dear remains,
His cold, insensate dust:—and even *this*
To view once more, and vent her anguished heart,
She early came; here to recall to mind
The cherished image of her sinless Friend,
His holy precepts and his spotless life,
His pious counsels, and that sacred love
Which warmed his breast, when, with compassion fired,
He looked with approbation on her deed,†
And said to Simon, "Seest thou this woman!
No water for my feet thou gavest me;
But she hath washed them with her precious tears,

---

* Luke, xxiii. 56. † Luke, vii. 44–47.

And wiped them with her hair. No kiss thou gav'st;
But since I entered in, she hath not ceased
To kiss my feet. Nor yet my head with oil
Didst thou anoint; but she with ointment hath
My feet anointed. Wherefore, unto thee
I say, her sins, though numerous, are forgiven."
These gracious words still glowed on memory's page,
And all the scenes—those fond, endearing scenes,
Where with her Lord she held communion sweet,
Passed in review—scenes, to return no more!
For "wicked hands" had crucified her Lord;
And now within the tomb, his lifeless form
Unconscious lay; all—*all* that now remained
Of him she loved. And still what ardent love
That sacred corse elicited!—But, oh!
If sorrow filled her heart, when on the Cross
She saw her friend expire; what speechless grief,
What anguish worse than death, must thrill her soul,
When with fond hope and love she sought his corse—
And sought in vain! The "stone was rolled away!"
Could we but see that frenzied countenance—
The soul-felt grief depicted in that face—
The disappointment and the blank despair
Her woeful mien presented, when she ran
To Simon and the "well beloved" John,
And in threnodial strains of speechless grief
Informed them—"They have ta'en away the Lord,

And (Oh, my soul!) we know not where he's laid!" *
Then came the two disciples, and surveyed
The vacant tomb, and learned the startling fact,
That though the "clothes" were left, the corse was gone!
This having learned, "they went to their own home."†
—Not so, the faithful MARY. Lingering still,
"Weeping she stood without;" and, as if hope,
A latent hope, still warmed her faithful heart,
With eyes o'erflowing, "she stooped down and looked
Into the sepulchre,"—if, haply, she
Might see once more the object of her love.
But now two angels meet her eager gaze,
Who ask her, why she weeps? And here, again,
Her bursting heart could only utterance give
To those same words, which seemed to sum her grief;
She makes the loss peculiarly her *own*—
Not, as at first, "*we* know not"—but "Because
They 've ta'en away *my* Lord, and *I* know not—‡
I know not where they 've laid him!"—Hapless one!
Oh! what a grief is here!—

Now turning back
She saw a man she knew not; but supposed
Most naturally, that he "the gardener" was:
He saw her tears, and kindly questioned her,
"Woman, why weepest thou? whom dost thou seek?"

---

* John, xx. 2. † John, xx. 10. ‡ John, xx. 13.

Intent on her benevolent design,
She still entreated, while a ray of hope
Yet gleamed before her vision, that she might
Obtain intelligence of him she loved,—
"If thou have borne him hence, O tell me where—
Where thou hast laid him; and give me the joy
To take possession of his loved remains!"

What could she more? What greater love display?
What deeper depth of sorrow, could the heart—
The human heart explore? What heavier weight
Of anguish could she bear, and yet survive?

But, oh! the Joy that followed in the train
Of *Grief* so withering! Ecstasy of Joy!
Joy, that no pen shall paint!—imparted, too,
By him she mourned, and by *one word* conveyed.
That well-known voice, those accents erst so sweet,
Now struck her ravished ear; and her own name—
The name so oft pronounced, in converse dear,
By that loved Friend whose loss she now deplored,
Fell on her ear, in cadence passing sweet,
In strains of love and tenderness, that thrilled
Her anguished heart: "Mary!" the Saviour said:
This word was all he uttered: this was all
Her kindred, sympathizing, feeling heart
Required. It told her all. And her reply,
"Rabboni!" spoke her soul, and owned her God!

DEDICATION.

WRITTEN IN THE ALBUM OF MISS EMMA S. C......

WHAT is an ALBUM? for what end designed?
—A store-house for the treasures of the MIND.
Here, then, let Intellect unfold her store,—
Let sun-lit Genius his rich offerings pour:
Let Science, laden with her classick spoils—
The well-earned meed of intellectual toils—
Bring forth her treasures, and impart her store,
To swell these pages with her richest lore.

Does EMMA relish intellectual food?—
Then never let the untaught mind intrude
To blot these pages:—let the grovelling soul—
(Content to reach his own terrestrial goal,)
Presume not once, with bold *Icarean* flight,[13]
To soar aloft to proud Parnassus' height;
Nor with a low-born thought to desecrate
Thine *Album*, destined to a nobler fate.

Let wisdom shine conspicuous on each page;
Let no unmeaning sentiments engage
The minds of those, who humbly seek for fame,
By wreathing laurels round a poet's name.

What nobler theme, amid the things of earth,
Can human reason grasp, than MENTAL WORTH?
What richer gem to human kind is given,
Than MIND, the precious gift of bounteous Heaven?

Corporeal excellence may charm a while,
Beauty and wit may sparkle, and beguile;
Science may dazzle, with a meteor glare,
Philosophy erect her throne in air:—

Reason may boast her all-controlling power,
And towering Genius reign, his transient hour;
But heaven-born MIND her onward course shall run,—
In deathless glory shall out-live the sun!

When earthly grandeur fades, and all things nod,—
When 'Nature trembles to the Throne of God,'—
This EMANATION from creation's Sire,
Shall soar aloft, unscathed, o'er all creation's pyre!

MARY.

(WRITTEN IN THE ALBUM OF MISS MARY E.....)

AT MARY's call, my tuneful muse essays
  Once more to mount Parnassus' lofty height;
Not with a view to win the poet's bays,
  But, aid MARIA in her heaven-ward flight.

Whether *Maria*, .Greek and Roman name,—
  Marie, French,—or *Mary*, Anglo-phrase;
Or whether *Miriam*, as in Hebrew fame,—
  The name is *one*, and claims no common praise.

O may the ancient *Marys* hold to view
  A pattern for your aim. *Mary*, the Bless'd—
The Virgin-mother, to her Joseph true,
  Excelled in faith, with grief and shame oppress'd.

May *Magdalene's* penitence be thine,
  A contrite sinner at Immanuel's seat;
And with the humble *Mary* may you shine
  As with your tears you lave the Saviour's feet!

With *Mary*, too,—sister of Martha dear,—
Choose "that good part," which none can take away;
Let gratitude and love and holy fear
  Inspire your breast, and point your heaven-ward way!

And "early to the sepulchre" repair,
  With the two *Marys*, at the dawn of day;
And lay, of Love the willing offering, there,
  And "see the place, where" your Redeemer "lay."

Marys of modern times, we too may name,
  Of shining Virtues, and of Fate severe;
Those, if you emulate, will swell your fame,—
  This, if you scan, may cause the flowing tear.

Marie, spouse of Gallia's hapless king,
  Doomed to the guillotine, in Terror's reign;—
Her social virtues well might virgins sing,—
  Her timeless doom must thrill each heart with pain!

And Scotia's *Mary*, too, of glowing charms
  A selfish votary at ambition's shrine,—
Shared in distress, amid a State's alarms,—
  While vice and virtue round her heart entwine.

Mary, Britannia's rigid, bigot Queen,
  May also give instruction by her reign;
From her *career of blood*, 't is clearly seen,
  Religion *thus* no proselytes can gain!

Then while the *good* you choose, the *evil* shun;
  Grow wise, by monitory lessons given;—
That when your destined race on earth is run,
  Yours be the Crown, in yonder glorious Heaven!

DEDICATION.

WRITTEN IN THE ALBUM OF MISS HANNAH ELIZA W.

Another Album?—yes, *Eliza* sues:
Once more awake! my dormant, slumbering Muse!
Inspire my breast, and tune my tuneless lyre,
With Latian symphony, and Attick fire!

None sues in vain:—Clorinda and Aurelia,
Annette and Susan, Angeline and Celia,
Have sued, and won;—then why may not *Eliza*
Claim a rich guerdon, that shall well suffice ye?

But cease the light and trifling strain,
The grave, didactick theme pursue;
To win the mind—the heart to gain,
The sober strain of truth renew.

In Heaven the theme began;
To earth with kind intent it came;
And timely lends its genial flame
A light to erring man.

Celestial Truth!
In blooming youth,
Inspire Eliza's heart, and point her way
To realms of Love,
In worlds above,
Thy native mansions of unclouded day!

Religion, holy flame of heavenly birth,
With ceaseless fervour in your bosom glow;
Not frantick zeal, that oft deforms our earth,
Prelusive source of our severest woe!

Virtue, the radiant daughter of the skies,
Deign to embrace you with her vestal zone;
Be it your aim to win this peerless prize,
No earthly treasure can whose loss atone.

Let modesty and mental worth
Adorn your every grace;
Worthless are all the gems of earth,
A peerless form—a faultless face—
Where modesty and mental worth
No friendly eye can trace.

Then let discretion rule the hour,—
Religion burn with purest flame;—
Stern Virtue lend her loveliest power,
And reason lawless passion tame.

When all externals fade,
And works of art decay;
When noblest fabricks pride has made,

In long oblivion lay;
Mind shall endure,
Angelick—pure—
And rise to endless day.

Then in this mental Register,
Let no unworthy thought intrude;
Be every line, inserted here,
Promotive only of thy good.

Oft does the grovelling mind,
Ambitious only to inscribe a name—
Write in an Album, with the hope of fame,
Words,—to their meaning, blind.

Not so, *his* mind, whom classick light illumes;
He would Instruction with his language blend:—
He knows the *Album's meaning;* and presumes
That mental food alone can sate his friend.

Appreciate, then, the scholar's lays,
The poet's garland duly prize;
But strive to let the christian's praise
Secure thy welcome in the skies!

Pure mental worth,
Scarce prized on earth,
Shall live, 'mid matter into ruin hurled;
And heaven-born MIND,
By grace refined,
Shall soar, 'midst seraph shouts, to yon empyreal world!

TO LOUISA.

ANNIVERSARY MONODY; MAY 30.

[Written in sickness.]

WITH faltering hand, I take my lyre once more,
  To sing *Louisa's* love—*Louisa's* truth:—
While I still linger on this mortal shore,
  No change shall shake the affection of my youth.

To thee, my Love, my earliest vows were paid;
  To thee my heart, in changeless truth, shall tend;
Nor, till I pass the vale of Death's dark shade,
  Shall thy *Lorenzo's* pure affection end.

For two and twenty years,—in weal and woe
  Alternate,—has our earthly journey run;
And ours has been the happiness to know,
  That EACH was faithful as *the untiring sun.*

How oft have we beheld, in this brief space,
  Without regret, life's pantomimick play;—
The proud—the great—all rise in glory's race,
  To win earth's laurels, for—*a transient day!*

Our happier lot, in humbler sphere, was cast;
  At *Home*, our happiness was mainly sought;
And of misfortune though we 've felt the blast,
  'T was richer still, than *fame*, with virtue bought.

Domestick peace has blessed our social hearth,
  And competence has crowned our frugal board;
And health's sweet voice, the richest boon of earth,
  Has called forth praise to our all-bounteous Lord.

But health—and strength—and buoyant spirits flee;
  By feeble tenure, holds *Lorenzo* life!
Louisa asks *one more memorial :*—She
  May read this Token, when—*my widowed wife !*—

For, change must come!—change marks the tide of life;—
  And now, the zenith of our day we 've gained;
Our occidental sun, with glory rife,
  God grant, may set—by lurid clouds unstained!

O, Jesus! Saviour, whose abounding grace
  Hath led us to devote ourselves to Thee;
Still grant thine aid, to run the heaven-ward race,
  Till Thou from earthly dross our spirits free.

And when thou call'st thine erring servant home,
  May he with joy put off this load of clay;
And may *Louisa*, and her children, come,
  To join *Lorenzo* in the realms of Day.

TO A BELOVED DAUGHTER.

ON HER BIRTH-DAY; NOVEMBER 29.

May this, Marie's natal day,
Auspicious prove;—and may each year
Revolving, on Time's rapid way,
Insure thee peace, and bliss sincere.

Each temporal blessing, still, to gain,
And keep thy mind in tranquil rest;
No moral guilt thy soul must stain,
To drive complacence from thy breast.

Oh, may'st thou ever find delight,
In Virtue's path, and Wisdom's ways,
Nor let the lures of sin's drear night,
Ensnare thy heart in Error's maze.

The joys of earth soon pass away!
Then, seek that bliss, which never dies:
Eternal joys, that ne'er decay,
Faith holds to view in yonder skies.

Our barque is launched on stormy seas!—
Soon—*soon*, shall earthly trials end;
Then may we reach our port in peace,—
Enter that REST, where sorrows cease,—
Received by CHRIST, the UNIVERSAL FRIEND.

SOLITARY MUSINGS.[14]

ADDRESSED TO A DISTANT FRIEND.

O, COULD my lips with equal warmth express
The glowing thoughts, which thrill this feeling heart,
Then might ELVIRA hope this page to find
Replete with language not devoid of sense.
But, ah, how vain are *words*, to speak the ***heart!***
The bosom swells with thoughts, which bid defiance
To cold and formal verbiage. Kindred souls
In unison will meet, and hold communion;
And the rapt spirit's voice, unto the voice
Of ravished spirit, in ethereal tone
Will speak responsive, audible to none
But kindred spirit!—Such are *thine* and *mine.*
Elvira, yes:—why should it not be thus,
That souls like ours, too sensitive for earth,
Should recognise affinity?

Full late,
Too late, indeed, we found each other here!
From the same generous stock we claim descent·
Our fortunes not unlike; and less unlike
Our discipline in sad Affliction's school!
And farther still, I trust, the likeness holds—

Both are recipients of JESUS' love.
Then, while we sojourn in this vale of tears,
Well may we bear the *Cross;* nor hopeless mourn,
If, past Death's vale, the blissful *Crown* be ours.

Memory, with all her busy train, awakes,
And calls in sad review the glowing scenes
Of years long past!—years, how diversified
With joy and grief, pain—pleasure—weal, and woe!
Ye blissful ages, run!—relieve my sight—
Point through the vista of past rolling years,
And let me catch, of Joy and Misery
The shadowy forms!

All—*all*, alas! are fled!
In youth, nor want I knew:—in infancy,
In childhood, parents' care—fraternal love—
Each wish anticipated, and each want
By kindly providence prevented.

All—
My Mother and my three loved Sisters—all,
Beneath the grasp of Death's prime minister,
A slow *consumption*, withered! And the rest,
That of my hapless Family remained,—
A Father, more than loved, revered—adored—
A Brother, rendered dear by every grace
That can exalt our nature, soon were called
To tread the path to Death's oblivious bourn!
—*Oblivious*, did I say? Faith holds a lamp

Which lights the sombre gloom, and darts a ray
To *Calvary's* height; and thence it radiates
The all-pervasive beams shot from the Cross—
The sun of Righteousness! Here, then, is Light,
Whose rays the midnight darkness of the tomb
Can ne'er obstruct.

Oh, lift the note of praise
To our salvation's Captain—Lamb of God,
Immaculate and pure, the Paschal Lamb—
IMMANUEL—God with us!

Yet, human note
How vain—how feeble—how inadequate
To render equal praise! "Thine be the hymn
That rolls its sacred tide along the realms
Of upper day!"

And shall we join that lay—
That heavenly strain—and hymn the God TRIUNE!
Roll on, ye wheels of time! I would not stay—
I would not linger in this nether sphere.
—Health ne'er was mine:—In vain I've wooed the Dame;
And life, without her, scarce deserves the name.
Then what, of earth, remains for me to prize?
Aloft I soar, and claim my native skies.
My buried kindred pioneer the way,
And hail me welcome to the realms of day;
Point to the pathway they through faith have trod,
To join in choral praise around the throne of GOD!

The succeeding poem is the effusion of that dear child, who has already been introduced to the reader. The feelings of a Father would not permit him to withold it from this volume. It can hardly fail to find a response in the breast of every Parent.

TO MY FATHER,

DISTANT FROM HOME.

FATHER! thou art far away,
On thy daughter's natal day;
In the stranger's distant land,
Separated from that band
Of loving hearts, who often pray
For blessings on thy lonely way;
And breathe the wish, that thou may'st roam,
Back to thy own mountain home.

FATHER! by that home's dear hearth,
Joyless sound the tones of mirth;
And the tuneful voice of song
Floating mournfully along,—

Minds us of thy absent face,
Of thy dreary, vacant place;
And the gushing tear-drops start,
From the fount of each warm heart!

FATHER! from the land and sea,—.
Gathered to our home so free,
Will our broken household chain
Meet with *all* its links again?
They who, in their childhood's bliss,
Shared the same fond Mother's kiss,
Will they, (ne'er again to roam,)
Meet in our own youthful home?

FATHER! yes, to part no more,
On a waveless, peaceful shore,
ALL the links of that dear chain,
Scattered, shall unite again;
Meet to join the tide of song,
Flowing gloriously along;
To the ***Lamb***, who dwells above,
IN OUR BEAUTEOUS HOME OF LOVE.

LOUISA.

Millington, Ct., Jan. 7.

CONSOLATORY REFLECTIONS.

A FRIENDLY TRIBUTE, INSCRIBED TO MRS. P. E. P..., OF SAVANNAH, GEORGIA; ON THE DEATH OF HER SON.

I have seen his ways, and I will heal him; I will lead him also, and restore comforts to him, and to his mourners. ISAIAH, LVII. 18.

ONE placid truth Philosophy may teach :—
Divide our burden, and more light our load
Will prove for our support. And as we find
Relief, when others' aid is proffered us,
So, in the weight of sorrows, that full oft
Oppress us in our pilgrimage of life,
Commiseration may impart relief,
And heartfelt sympathy our cares divide :—
True sympathy, alas! how rarely felt!
How few the hearts that own its genial sway!

Tell me of sympathy?—'T is mockery, all,
Unless the heart be torn with kindred grief!
Misanthropy as well might claim to share
In *Love for fellow man.* None but the hear'

With grief oppressed—with anguish torn—can feel
For those oppressed with grief and sorrow's weight.

And am I, then, instructed for the task—
The friendly office? May I sympathize
With thee, my sister?—may I pour the balm—
The heavenly balm of sympathetick grief?—
I, who remain alone—of all my House
The sole surviver?—I, a withered trunk—
Like mountain pine, oft with the lightning scathed,
A monument of sparing mercy, saved,—
A beacon to the circumjacent world!
May I approach thee, sister-mourner,—I,
Thy brother, in the bond of christian love,—
Thy brother-mourner, taught in sorrow's school,
And disciplined in stern Affliction's lore?
Shall I thus come; and as a friend, essay
To lead thy mind to rest? The work, ere now,
Perchance, is done: thy father's richer mind,
His deeper views, his far superior lore
In christian treasures, may prevent the task
Which I, thy sympathizing friend, though late,
Would cheerfully perform; and supersede
The need of my sincere, though faint, attempt.

But grant my task superfluous: still I feel
A sweet assurance, that my sister's heart
Will fail not to appreciate the love,
The fellow-feeling, that hath prompted me

To write this friendly tribute; to evince
That I can feel for others in distress,
Participate their pains, and share their grief.

Since first I learned *Lysander's* early doom,
I 've been with thee in spirit; and my heart
Has bled with thine, and in thy anguish shared.
And when I *traced a line to deck the stone*
Which designates his grave, I then resolved
To tell *his Mother* how I felt for her,
And prove ELVIRA's sympathizing friend.

How deep, how holy is a *Mother's* grief!
"A Mother's sorrows cannot be conceived
But by a Mother." Yet, a Father's heart
Is not insensate; if that Father's heart—
A husband's also—has, like mine, been riven,
When—mourning our lost cherub—I beheld
Louisa's tears bedew her *William's* grave!
Then deem me not intrusive. Do not think
I feign to *feel*, while yet my heart is cold,
And mock thy sorrows with dissembled grief.
No—lovely mourner! with the healing balm
Of christian sympathy, I come to thee.

Philosophy, I said, one truth may teach:
But, ah, the dictates of philosophy,—
How cold, how cheerless, if but once compared
With mild RELIGION's heaven-descended Light!

Let this mild light shine inward, and pervade
The heart's recesses: let it point the way
To Calvary's height, and there disclose the Lamb—
The expiation of all moral sin.
See our Religion's Founder: hear his voice—
His gentle accents, breathing Love and Peace;
And bringing consolation to the heart
Of those, who mourn their children's early doom:—
"Permit these little ones to come to me;
For Heaven's kingdom is of such composed."*
"'T is not your heavenly Father's will, that one
Of these should perish."†

Comfort, then, thy heart
With this divine assurance, this behest;
For He is faithful—He is strong to save,
Who gave the promise. Wherefore dost thou weep?
Thy child is safe—safe in his Saviour's arms.
Though he precede thee to the realms of bliss,
From him thy separation is but brief.
And think, oh, think, how many ills of earth,
How many pains, and soul-polluting sins
He has escaped, by being thus recalled.

Soon thou wilt follow, sister-mourner! soon;
And join thy babe in yon celestial sphere.

---

* St. Luke, xviii. 16. † St. Matt. xviii. 14.

For, at the longest, short our day of life;
And soon, full soon, will life's probation close!
Though clouds and darkness circumvolve the Throne
Of the ETERNAL; and his ways to us
Inscrutable appear,—*His ways are right.*

Then let us bow submissive to his will;
His laws obey; take comfort from his word;
Pursue the path of duty; run the race
Before us set, with patience; all our time
Appointed, patient wait, till our change come.
Then, rich in faith, rich in the Saviour's love,
And borne aloft on Hope's seraphick wing,
May we, with joy, resign our 'dust to dust;'
Proclaim *Adieu* to these terrestrial scenes;
Ascend to realms of bliss, to join our friends—
Our 'loved and lost of earth,'—and reunite
To part no more; where death no more shall sport
With our endearments, where no tears shall flow;
But Peace, and Joy, and Love, unceasing reign!

Yet, while we linger in this drear sojourn,
And *loved ones*, dear as life, are from us torn;
Can feeble nature view their early bier,
And, lost to feeling, stay the gushing tear?
Ah, no,—'t is nature's voice! the heart o'erflows,
And tears, alone, the heart-felt wound can close!
Nor will such grief displease that Holy Guest,
Whose precious tears *the Grave of* LAZARUS *blest.*

DIRGE.

COMMEMORATIVE OF MRS. LYDIA FOSTER GREEN; CONSORT OF MR. ANSON GREEN OF NEW YORK; WHO DIED AT GREENPORT, LONG ISLAND, MAY 6, 1837.

Affectionately inscribed to the bereaved PARTNER, *the surviving* PARENT, *and the* BROTHERS *and* SISTERS *of the* DECEASED.

"———————— Smitten Friends
Are angels sent on errands full of LOVE:
For us they languish, and for us they die!"

IN Death's unbounded realm, no order reigns;
No station, sex, or age, his hand restrains.
Athletick manhood falls, his helpless prize,
Nor does he heed the feeble infant's cries.
Connubial Love, the dearest tie of life,
No shield opposes to his ruthless strife!

Life's day is bright:—o'erflows the cup of joy,
And pleasure reigns, which seems each sense to cloy.
Too soon, alas! this day is changed to night;
Death's summons comes, the fairest scene to blight!

Stern, though capricious, see the tyrant come:
He shuns the hoary head, ripe for the tomb,
And smites the graceful youth,—the blooming boy,
The mother's darling, and the father's joy.
The heaven-defying infidel he spares,
And takes the Vestal, kneeling at her prayers:
Now leaves the mother,—strikes the sinless child,
While on her bosom it serenely smiled:
Anon he leaves that spotless Innocent,
Which to its parent was so lately lent,
And smites the mother!—

Oh, thou righteous God!
This blow is *ours*—we feel thy vengeful rod!
Vengeful?—ah, no:—Thy holy name is LOVE;
Then naught but MERCY cometh from above.
Although inscrutable to mortal sight,
Thy ways, in reason's view, must all be right:
Thy servant Death thy wise behest obeys,
And where would REASON counteract his ways?
Oh, may thy Judgments rouse to thought the soul,
And let bereavement grief's pure flood control!

I would not check, too rigidly, the tear,
That freely flows o'er LYDIA's early bier,
The sadness of the countenance imparts
Divine instruction to our rebel hearts.

Yet, while we mourn, let not our hearts rebel;
We yield to God, the friend we loved so well;—
Her dust to dust,—her spirit to its God,—
And with submission bow, and kiss the rod!

Why one is taken, and another left,—
Why some survive—of all their friends bereft;—
Why such diversity through life obtains,—
Why one is blest—another heir to pains;—
Why this abounds in wealth beyond control,
And cheerless penury chills the other's soul;
Why one on his luxurious couch may sleep,
And one is fated but to wake, and weep;—
Why one may revel on his countless hoard,
And one just *vegetates*, at his lean board;—
'T is not revealed to man:—nor would we know
The destined boundaries of our weal, or woe!
Infinite Mercy kindly hid from man,
A previous knowledge of the Almighty's plan:
For, sure, in mercy is that stroke concealed,
Which antedates our misery, if revealed.

Thou widowed *Mother!* whose too feeling heart
Has oft been pierced with grief's envenomed dart;
Ye gentle *Sisters*, and ye *Brothers* dear,
Who oft have shed affliction's scalding tear;
And thou bereaved *Husband*, from whose side,
Insatiate Death has torn a youthful bride;—

Permit your kinsman, versed in sorrow's lore,
With mingling tears, the cup of Joy to pour.
And that my tears in pure condolement flow,
Ye, who best know *me*, cannot fail to know:
Misfortune's child—Affliction's favourite son—
Since first my pilgrimage on earth begun—
I well may feel, and weep for others' woe;—
But, freed from suffering, who can pity know?
Or, how can one, who never knew a smart,
Give to distress a sympathizing heart?

Shall I essay to pour the healing balm,
And sorrow's whelming wave attempt to calm?—
—I own the TASK:—but, guided by that ray,
Which sweetly gleams from realms of upper day,
I take thee, widowed Mother! to thy child,
Who late on thee, in health, serenely smiled;
And you, dear sisters—brothers—husband, all,
Come, raise with me your LYDIA's funeral pall,
That shrouds from sight, her graceful, faded form,
And spreads a banquet for the insatiate worm!
Behold that lovely child—that sister—bride—
Clad for the tomb! while Death, in conscious pride,
Smiles o'er his victim, with exulting reign,
And vainly clanks his agonizing chain!
Yes, vainly clanks it:—vain that tyrant's power,
Who sways a sceptre scarce one transient hour.

—See! see, his Conqueror comes! the Incarnate God,
Who once "the wine-press of God's vengeance trod;"*
Who nailed our sins to the accursed tree,
Unnumbered souls from sin's dire curse to free;
Descending thence, these gloomy confines trod,
Then soared triumphant to his Father God:—
Thus, conquering Death and Hell, and all his foes,
The Almighty CAPTAIN of SALVATION rose!

And may not she, who meekly bore his Cross,
Compared with which, all else esteemed but loss;
Who gave her youth, her life, her soul, to God,
And wisdom learned from his paternal rod;
Who cast the joys of earth beneath her feet,
And aimed alone to win in heaven a seat;—
May she not hope, that heavenly rest to gain,
Where endless joy succeeds to mortal pain?

Ye Mourners! here, come taste your cup of Joy,
Which not the dregs of earth can e'er alloy.
Here rests your Hope:—In renovated bloom,
Your LYDIA's form shall burst this lurid tomb;
Like its "FIRST FRUITS,"† in deathless beauty rise,
To dwell with Christ her Lord above the skies.

---

* Rev. xix, 15. † 1 Cor. xv, 20.

TO ELVIRA.

ON THE DEATH OF HER BELOVED SISTER, MRS. LYDIA F. GREEN

O, SISTER! dry that falling tear,
For sister *Lydia*—called away
From earthly pains, to yon bright sphere,
The blissful realms of endless day.

I know thy grief—I know thy pain—
I, too, have felt affliction's smart;
But let calm resignation reign,
And bland Religion cheer thy heart.

Hast thou not given thyself to God?—
Dost thou not own his ways are right?—
Is it not thine to *kiss the rod*,
Which seems thy every Joy to blight?

My Sister's anguish let me share,
Thy sorrows all, let me divide;
Thy nameless griefs I freely bear—
I sail with thee on misery's tide!

Oh, let us think, in mercy mild
Our Heavenly Father seems to chide;
For Love paternal owns his child,
When grace subdues rebellious pride.

Alas! that pride should swell a worm—
  A helpless creature of a day:—
Too much we prize this earth-born form,
  That hastes so quickly to decay!

Yes, sister! soon thy feeble frame
  Must fall—the wreck of mortal pain;—
But, praise to God! through JESUS' name,
  Thy stainless SOUL shall *rest* obtain.

And must thou go?—Thy brother's tear,
  Warm from a faithful, feeling heart,
Shall, unrestrained, flow o'er thy bier,
  When death, relentless, bids us part!

The dreary confines of the tomb
  Were by our bless'd Redeemer trod;
Who, rising thence, in deathless bloom,
  Soared to the bosom of his God!

Thy sister, first, has sought the skies,
  And left us here a while to mourn;
Through JESUS' love, we soon shall rise,
  Triumphant o'er Death's lurid bourn.

Then, sister! dry that scalding tear,
  For *Lydia*, early called away:—
She hails thee, from yon blissful sphere,
  To join her in ETERNAL DAY.

May, 1837.

ELEGY;

COMMEMORATIVE OF MRS. ELIZABETH B. WILLEY, OF EAST HADDAM, CONN.; WIFE OF MR. WILLIAM M. WILLEY, AND DAUGHTER OF THE LATE MR. NOADIAH EMMONS.

Affectionately inscribed to her Mother and other surviving friends.

———the memory of joys that are past; pleasant and mournful to the soul!—OSSIAN.

SCENES of the PAST! how dear in memory's shrine!
How bright your visions still in fancy shine!
With rapt delight, I call to mind the past,
And fondly wish your pictured scenes may last.
But, ah! like summer clouds that paint the sky,
Dissolved in air, they prematurely fly!
An emblem sad, of all on earth we prize,
Whose brief existence mocks our longing eyes.
Thus fancied bliss the ravished soul employs,
Then proves how vain are earth's most cherished joys;
And, while we seem to embrace the valued prize,
Eludes our grasp, and, like a meteor, flies!

Like vernal sun, arose ELIZA's morn,
And brilliant prospects her bright sky adorn;

Youth, health and beauty gem her flowery way,
And all give promise of a splendid day;
Nature and art in sweet embrace conspire,
And lend their aid to sate each pure desire;
Parental love and love fraternal join,
And general friendship's dearest ties combine,
With one accord, to beautify her soul,
And train her mental powers with mild control.
While o'er her mind fair science held her sway,
Religion's light diffused its genial ray.
Thus sacred love and plastick art conspire,
To mend the heart, and consecrate desire.
'Tis thus the mind is formed, with fondest care,
In purest bliss domestick life to share;
To taste the transports of connubial joy,
To gratify each wish, but never cloy;
The thoughts, desires, affections to control,
And train for heavenly bliss the labouring soul.

Such was ELIZA's lot. And years long past
Come fresh to mind, without a cloud o'ercast;
And faithful memory paints a scene to view,
Which, ever-during, seems for ever new.
Long have I laboured in the cause of Youth,
With ardent wish to store their minds with truth;
To fit them to adorn earth's highest sphere,
And "temples for the Holy Spirit" rear.

The sweet reflection, that I may have been,
In the Almighty's hand, an humble mean
Of forming nascent minds for bliss above,
By teaching them the depths of JESUS' love
Is richest recompense for pains and cares
Bestowed, to train for life salvation's heirs.
And when my pupils leave this vale of tears,
(Of whom *Eliza* was, in by-gone years—)
Affectionate remembrance loves to trace
Their mental worth, and each endearing grace.
Though now removed from that romantick scene,
Where, on yon classick Mount, I long had been;
What dear associations still combine
To endear that spot, and round fond memory twine!
ELIZA, there, among the female train,
Who flocked to ACADEMUS' halls, to gain
The sparkling gems of science' ample store,
Imbued her mind with learning's varied lore.
And there, in favouring auspices, her life
Led to the endearing station of a wife,
Where she, in holy matrimonial tie,
Dwelt,—when I left to seek a milder sky,
When, to my loved PARNASSUS bade farewell,
And here, in "Penn's throng'd city," came to dwell.
There, too, her Father dwelt—friend of my youth—
A friend, held dear by ties of sacred truth:—
He, first, was called to meet his Judge, above,
Though bound to earth by many a tie of love.

Soon—soon, Eliza follows in the train,
Thus *twice the peace of numerous friends is slain!**
A widowed mother, sisters, brothers dear,
And stricken husband, shed affection's tear!
And infant children—words, alas! how vain
Their loss to paint, or mitigate their pain!
A *Mother's* death creates an aching void
Earth ne'er can fill!—earth's bliss seems all destroyed!
The yawning chasm no length of years can close,
Ev'n sympathy seems but to awake our woes!
Ye, who have lost a tender *Mother*, say—
Can time efface the misery of that day,
When her loved form was ravished from your sight,
And left you, *orphans*, in this world's drear night!
And can condolence check the flowing tear?—
Doth it not, oft, but mockery appear?
Time's lenient hand may moderate our grief;
But nothing earthly yields entire relief.
The Gospel's light, alone, unfolds a ray,
Bright from the precincts of immortal day,
Which leads us to repose on God's dear Son,
And say, submissively, "Thy will be done;"
Inspires with hope, to meet in realms above,
And claim re-union with the friends we love.
This HOPE, that we will join our friends once more,
In blissful union, on the heavenly shore,

---

* Thy shafts flew twice, and twice my peace was slain!—Dr. Young

May reconcile us to bereavement, here,
And rule, with just control, affliction's tear:
And, thus, our tears may flow o'er kindred, dead,
Approved of Him, who tears for *Lazarus* shed.

Religion's purer light dispels the gloom,
Which untaught reason spread around the tomb.
Before the SAVIOUR hallowed that drear bed,
All hope was buried with th' unconscious dead:
When He emerged from that sepulchral night,
LIFE, IMMORTALITY, were brought to light!
Then, hope was given, that those in CHRIST who sleep,
Death could no more in lasting bondage keep;
But in the SAVIOUR's image they should rise,
To reign with Him, in bliss beyond the skies.
His friendly voice pronounced the *mourners* blest;—
For, comfort they shall find, and heavenly rest.*
Rich consolations in God's word abound;—
For *widows*, *orphans*, joy and peace are found.†

This state of trial, this probation-day;
At longest, brief—full soon will pass away—
The rudiments of being!—This short space
Is here allotted us, a DAY of GRACE;
Which, if in wisdom's ways this day we spend,
Prepares for blessedness that ne'er will end.

---

* St. Matt v. 4.

† Jer. xlix. 11.—Ps. lxviii. 5., *etc.*

Bereaved Mourners! ye, who feel the rod,
Bear it with joy:—behold your Saviour, God,
Who bore his cross;—and hear his kind behest—
"Take up your cross, and follow me to rest."*
With such a Friend, O, never once despair,—
On Him cast all your burden—all your care:
The race, before you set, with patience run;
A crown of joy awaits your journey done.
Eliza, first, has gained that blest abode;—
Our dying friends but smooth the rugged road!†
—And, oh! the blissful hour! when we shall sail
O'er Jordan's wave, and far-off Canaan hail!
When, welcomed to th' exalted Saviour's Throne,
We join in praises to the Three in One;
And swell the tide of that angelick lay,
Which rolls unceasing through the realms of day!

---

* St. Matt. xi. 29.

† Our dying friends are pioneers to smooth
The rugged pass to death!—Dr. Young.

DITHYRAMBICK.[15]

RESPECTFULLY INSCRIBED TO THE EDITOR OF THE "NEW YORK WEEKLY MESSENGER."

Variety 's the very spice of life.—COWPER.
Laugh where we must; be candid where we can.—POPE.

THOUGH no *Free-Mason*, still I come,
At thy "grand hailing sign;"—
And though no *scion* here may bloom,
Of the oft courted NINE.

For who can here,
In region drear,
So near the polar Zone,—
Of *Poesy's* ray
Feel the mild sway,
With *blood congealed to* STONE!

Yet while I sit on famed *Parnassus'* Mount,
Its inspiration I dare not disclaim,
Who oft have bathed in *Heliconia's* fount,
And vainly hoped to win a poet's name.

But what 's the use,
With brain obtuse,
To woo the coy, fastidious NINE?
As well the rose,
'Mid Arctick snows,
Might hope in *Flora's* train to shine!

Yet grateful will I prove,—
For I have won their love,—
And shared their favours, erst, in days, "lang syne;"
Then, haply, their control—
If I but call their roll—
May *perpetrate* a verse, and call it *mine*.

URANIA, muse divine! my thoughts inspire,
And lovely CLIO, lend thy wonted fire,
CALLIOPE,
MELPOMENE,
And POLYHYMNIA, join the tuneful choir;—
And TERPSICHORE, gay,
And comick THALIA,
ERATO, priestess at young Cupid's fane,
And sweet EUTERPE, swell the choral strain!

Behold, in lines just *nine*,
Your *novem nomina** shine,—

* Nine names.

An invocation, erst, by me designed;—
Whatever names ye bear,—
Whatever titles wear,—
Whatever office is to each assigned;
From realms of light descend,—
Your inspiration lend,—
Breathe into *matter* your ethereal *mind!*

But, why essay, with polished verse to please,
When only plain and business style I need?
My toil 's requited with an ample meed,
If only *Editorial toils* I ease.

The labours of the *Editorial Corps*
Full well I know :—and trifles light and brief,
To silence the "Compositor's" shrill roar
For "copy—copy,"—may afford relief.

To thee, my Friend, who caterest so sweetly,
For palates, appetites, and tastes fastidious;
Fain would I link my words and rhymes so neatly,
That I may not offend the most invidious.

And to thy kind inquiry, "what 's become of me?"
I answer civilly, and like a hero;—
As to my *corpus*, there remains yet some of me,
Though *vital warmth* is ten degrees *sub* Zero!

But to be serious—not to speak in figures,—
  My health is feeble—life is on the wane;
A warmer climate—ev'n among the "*niggers*"—
  Would much relieve these shivering limbs of pain.

I'd even quit Parnassus' height, and go
  To milder regions—a more genial clime;
Where I might bid adieu, for aye, to *snow*,
  And *thaw* where Sol pours torrid beams sublime!

But soon may SPRING return,
  With its reviving ray;
Life's flickering taper brighter burn,
  To cheer my lone and dreary way!

Then, may my feeble lays, once more,
  An entrance in thy columns find;
Lays, if not rife with classick lore,
  Yet worthy of a cultured mind.

Still, when I read the chastened lays,
  Which grace thy sheet, from "L. H. S.,"
Or seek in vain "OPHELIA'S" bays,
  Despair may well *this mind* depress!

To name but these, perhaps might seem
  Invidious, to that lovely sex;
"MARGARETTE McN.," and "A. E. M.,"
  And many more, *my muse* perplex.

Although I fail THEIR height to reach
  I still would never *recreant* prove;
And if my stanzas fail to *teach*,
  They show that I the MUSES love.

With the few talents God hath given,
  I may not frame an *Ethick Code*;
Yet I will trace the ways of Heaven,
  In a plain, humble

NEW YEAR'S ODE.

I.

How rapid, in his wild career,
Time wheels away the parting year,
  And brings this festal day;
An epoch for the thoughtful mind,
To cast a serious thought behind,
  And scan Life's devious way.

II.

How many precious souls have fled,—
Their bodies numbered with the dead,—
  Since last this day we hailed!
How many, o'er the gloomy bier,
Have poured of Grief the scalding tear,
  And "smitten friends" bewailed!

III.

How many in the mighty deep,
Have sunk in their long night of sleep,
  And found a watery grave!
The billowy surges' booming swell
Pealed o'er their heads the funeral knell,—
  Their winding-sheet—the wave!

IV.

Nor less has the devouring flame,
Whose rage no human skill can tame,
  Spread devastation round:—
And domes and spires, the pride of Art,
Late decorations of yon MART,[16]
  In ruins strew the ground!

V.

How many, in the wildering maze
Of specious sin's destructive ways,
  Pursue their mad career;
Despising reason's warning voice,
To make of *Death* and *Hell* their choice
  Which mock Contrition's tear!

VI.

And heathen darkness blinds the sight
Of myriads, lost in mental night,
  Where Superstition reigns;
While Moslem faith in thraldom binds
A countless host of heaven-born minds,
  With rank IMPOSTURE's chains!

VII.

Blest with the Gospel's purer ray,
By Faith we soar to realms of day,
  Nor dread a *rayless* tomb:
Its dreary confines JESUS trod,
And, rising thence, the INCARNATE GOD
  Dispelled its fearful gloom.

VIII.

Change marks the Year!—and Joy and Woe,
Alternate, visit all below,
  To crown Life's mingled bowl:
Dread Misery's lore by Heaven is sent,—
As Mercy's favours kindly lent,—
  To win the erring soul.

IX.

While we adore the bounteous hand,
That scatters blessings o'er our land,—
  The source of every good;
Oh, let our hearts Compassion warm,
The abodes of poverty to charm,
  And give the hungry food.

X.

And while our noblest strains aspire,
To emulate the angelick choir,
  Around the Throne of GOD;
Redeeming GRACE should wake our song,
And call forth praise from every tongue,
  For CHRIST's atoning blood!

Jan. 1836.

SPRING.[17]

Come, gentle SPRING! ethereal mildness, come.—THOMSON.

But WINTER, lingering, chills the lap of May.—GOLDSMITH.

———————————— Where art thou,
O SUN! Is the Sun turned recluse?—DR. YOUNG.

LONG have I waited the return of SPRING,
That I, once more, her genial reign might sing.
I wait in vain!—No genial Spring is here;
But *Winter's* sceptre rules the circling year!
A "variation," hence, to GOLDSMITH's tune,
For "Winter, lingering, chills the lap of" *June!*

Alas! for us, "inhabiters of Earth,"
That Astronomick *nostrums* e'er had birth!
That Herschel thus should fright *Selene's* folks,*
And palm on us a philosophick hoax![18]
Sirius has fled, and the mild *Pleiades*
Have, doubtless, plunged into the Tyrrhene seas;

---

* Greek Σελήνη, the moon.

For earth no more their grateful influence feels,
Sirius no longer barks, nor bites our heels.
Arcturus and *Orion*—all the van
Have left their homes, and gone to—Michigan!
The *Chambers of the South* are rented out
To *Ursa Major*, for a winter's rout!
The stars seem frightened; *Hocus pocus* dire
Has chilled the ardour of their quondam fire.
The *Milky way* congeals!—no cream can rise—
The *Dipper*, then, may well desert the skies!
The *Constellations* all, are struck *agog*,
Stirred up by Herschel's *telescopick Log!*
And *Luna's* "winged natives" stare with fright,
At such an influx of extraneous light!

When the bold wight, with his all-powerful glass,
Shall bring again such direful ills to pass,
Well may he curse the day when he was born,
And hang himself on *Luna's* longest HORN!
But let his genius compass nobler aims,
And warm our earth with artificial flames:
Could he but cause a lambent flame of gas
Through this our *polar atmosphere* to pass,
Or, with his *mammoth tube*, reflect a ray
Of *calorifick light* to warm our clay;
He thus, ev'n now, might partially atone
For all the mischief his self-will has done.

Would that the "man bats" had arisen, *en masse*,
And whelm'd with "melon rinds" the peering ass;
If his "discoveries" were to be the cause
Of *rigour*, counteracting nature's laws.

See its effects. The harbinger of Spring
Yon pretty *blue-bird*,—gladly would she sing;—
But vain th' attempt; she strives to ope her bill;—
How her teeth chatter! Lo, what accents shrill,
Widely diverse from her accustomed strain—
A doleful shriek, indicative of pain!

The lovely *red-breast*, too, with tearful eyes,
Holds up one foot—instead of singing, sighs!
The buoyant *sky-lark*, whose melodious voice
Was wont to make the groves and vales rejoice,—
What can he, now?—no concord marks his tune,
While winter's rigour chills the heart of JUNE!
And ev'n yon *raven*,—whose sonorous throat,
When free from frost, pours *one* harmonious note,—
No longer chanting his mellifluous "caw,"
With pain parturient, only brings forth—AWE!

On yonder side-hill, that regards the south,
See the poor *thrush*—her toes within her mouth!
She tries in vain to wake her feeble note,
As her chilled *digits* occupy her throat!

What woes, alas! the feathered tribe attend!—
When, *when*, O Herschel! shall their miseries end?

Pardon, dear readers, these my *swan-like* lays;—
Too *gelid* still,—I seek no poet's bays:
Indulging my propensity to rhyme,
I hail not Spring, *de facto*;—but the time,
The *date*, by which we note Time's onward way,
Would seem t' insure us from drear Winter's sway.
The precept, *carpe diem*, then, I'll heed;
And while a rhymer's vanity I feed,
The pledge I, whilom, gave, I thus redeem,
Lest of my promise I regardless seem;
And yield my labours to your just *assize*,
As not despairing yet to win the poet's prize.

June 20, 1836.

THE FETTERS OF COLUMBUS.

WHY in the breast does indignation rise
Unbidden?—why the involuntary tear
Course down the cheek of SENSIBILITY,
As we recount, even at this day remote,
Thy numerous wrongs, COLUMBUS! Thy exploits,
Thy matchless skill, thy daring enterprize
Have oft inspired the poet; and the page
Of sober history has inscribed thy name
In lineaments of light,—in characters,
Which, through all coming time, no WRONGS shall blot.

Wrongs, thou hast suffered; deep, abiding wrongs,
Which cannot be redressed.[19] But let the Muse,
Indignant, trace, in ***bold relief***, those WRONGS;
Disclose th' injustice, base ingratitude,—
The hardships, toils and injuries thou hast borne
From perjured royalty, insidious foes
And selfish rivals:—vile *ingratitude*,—
The vice peculiar to Republicks, called.

—But what Republick bears so foul a curse,
(Ev'n Rome and Athens may repel the charge—)
As that base Monarchy, and its worse *tools*,
Who listened to thy slanderers; and with rude
And sacrilegious hand, and perjured faith,
Infringed the sacred compact made with thee,
And ratified with due solemnity
By Spain's proud Queen, high-minded ISABEL.
—Long, *long* thy struggle!—Eight perplexing years
Thy suit was urged—thy patience tried—ere yet
O'er ignorance, philosophy prevailed,
And to thy prayer obtained the listening ear
Of Spain's united monarchs; who at length
"Supplied the barque, and bade Columbus sail!"

Thy native Genoa but ill repaid
That patriotism, which led thee, first, to seek
Her aid, and tender her thy services.
And feeble JOHN of Portugal refused
To lend his aid, and second thy desire
To give new splendour to his faded crown,
By aiding thine emprize:—yet meanly sought
To rob thee of thy glory, and by stealth
Obtain thy wished-for prize. But Heaven ordained
Far otherwise: for thee, for *thee* alone,
It was decreed, to track the pathless waste;
And in despite of boisterous elements
And the phenomenon of *nature's change*,[20]

Thy "reason steered—thy skill disarmed the gale;"
While feebler spirits cowered before the task,
And treachery's efforts met discomfiture.
Thy prescience led thee on:—thy puny fleet—
Thy *St. Maria, Pinta, Nigna*—sailed,
And rode, triumphant, o'er the boisterous deep,
Till *Guanahani* blessed thy longing sight:
And, safely landed on that barbarous strand,
A glad *Te Deum* rose from grateful hearts!
Here was the germ, whence all thy laurels spring.

Now grateful plaudits welcome thy return
To Palos:—but too soon Spain's haughty sons
Gave wanton rein to Envy: base self-love
And captious spleen ill brook'd that thou shouldst share
The honours and emoluments assured
By Spain's united crown. Oh, perfidy!
Ingratitude most base!—And must the Muse,
In after-ages, far remote, recount
This deed, most infamous in History's lore,
That, on a further visit to thy land—
Thine, by discovery—by compact *thine*—
Thy graceful limbs should wear the felon's chain,
And, at the mandate of an envious wretch,
Hispaniola's lord, thou shouldst be bound?
And, FETTERED *like a criminal*, return
To that ungrateful land, which, else, had won,

By thine exploits, a never-dying fame,
But which thy FETTERS stamp with *infamy!*

Thy violated rights were ne'er restored,
And basely were thy promised honours filched:
The remnant of thy useful life was spent
In fruitless efforts to redress thy wrongs.
But while possessed of *sound, disposing mind,*
Thou wast permitted to indite a WILL,
And designate thy son, Executor:[21]
"Go, FERDINAND, go bring my FETTERS here
Hang them in my apartment, where my eyes
May ever be delighted with the sight!
They are a precious treasure:—rich reward
For all my services! a Monarch's *Gift!*
A kingly present! pledge of royal faith!
A token of a Nation's Gratitude!
Here let them hang, to bless my ardent gaze,
And fix within my heart a Monarch's love!
And when my 'dust to dust' thou shalt commit,
So highly do I prize this royal gift,
O, let it not be sundered from my heart;
But let my FETTERS share my peaceful grave!"
—A WILL, indeed! A scorching *epitaph*
For *punick faith*—for *perjured royalty!*

Yet, though COLUMBUS sleeps, his *name* shall live,
And Spain's proud aristocracy outlive.

Though Florentine Vespucius stole his name,[22]
COLUMBIA still shall grace the Roll of Fame!
This name is dear to every patriot breast;—
Why should *injustice* blot it from our crest?
In the corrupted customs of this world,
Too oft is VIRTUE from her zenith hurled!
Vice, oft triumphant, holds remorseless sway;
But Heaven has in reserve a glorious day,
"To bring forth all the deeds of men to light,
And every one, as he deserves, requite."
Then *fetters* shall COLUMBUS gall no more;
But, there, redressed for all the wrongs he bore,
His sainted spirit shall in glory reign,
While his malignant foes are doomed to misery's chain

POEMS;

HOMEWARD BOUND

INSCRIBED TO LOUISA.

BORNE on affection's wing, I haste
  Back to my native hills again;
Hope of the *future*, cheers the *past*—
  I launch upon the wide-spread main!

Anxious to lay this painful head
  On my LOUISA's faithful breast,
I leave this distant, *lonely* bed,
  To greet my long-loved HOME OF REST.

For there, a wife and children dear,
  With anxious longing, look for me;
Then will the INVALID not fear
  Once more to brave the treacherous sea.

Propitious breezes! swell the sail,
  And waft me to my welcome Home;
Though borne, alas! on every gale,
  A summons greets me from the tomb

The time is brief I linger here;—
  Probation's day is well-nigh sped;
I hail the peaceful moment near,
  Which numbers me among the dead!—

All my appointed time I'll wait,
  Contented still to linger here;
If, haply, in this trial-state,
  My wife and children I may cheer:—

For YE, indeed, are all the ties,
  That bind me to this heartless earth;—
Naught else have I, beneath the skies,—
  Child of affliction, from my birth!

But, dear LOUISA! Heaven hath rest
  For us, and ours, which ne'er will end;
For in the mansions of the Blest,
  We have an everlasting Friend.

If we our Father's WILL perform,
  We'll join our friends in upper skies;
When all of earth,—escaped the storm,—
  Shall from earth's EMPYROSIS rise!

"Now launch the boat upon the wave,
  The wind is blowing off the shore;"
Again the watery world I brave—
  I seek my distant HOME once more.

Philadelphia, October, 1, 1839.

THE VOICE OF FRIENDSHIP; BREATHED RESPONSIVE.[23]

TO MISS A. E. M.

Non ignara mali, miseris succurrere disco.—VIRGIL.

"Oh, WOMAN'S heart is like the rose,
That glows beneath the tropick's flame;
That blooms as sweet 'mid northern snows,
For ever lovely, and the same."

BE this my motto:—and let deathless praise
Await the author of that peerless verse!
I rather would have penned that sentiment,
Than have achieved the deeds, which stamp the name
Of CÆSAR, *brave;* or ALEXANDER, *great!*
Once an illiberal, churlish poet said
Frailty, thy name is woman. And his fame
Ranks high on page poetick, who thus durst
Proscribe the gentle sex;—But I will dare
(An humble poet, scarcely known to fame—)
Thus to *redeem* the sentiment; and write
WOMAN, *thy name is* LOVE!

For, in what place,
What state, what exigence, what trying scene,

Where love, benevolence, or sympathy,
Or deed of noble daring, was required,
Was *not* there found this angel-minister—
This holy priestess of HUMANITY!

WHO waited on the *Saviour*; laved his feet
With tears—rich tears, streams from compassion's fount,—
And wiped them with her hair? WHO brake the box
Of precious ointment, and upon his head—
His sacred head, its costly contents poured?
Who at the *Cross* last lingers, to bewail
Her murdered Saviour? Who prevents the dawn,
And, on the wings of love, to see her Lord,
Comes first unto the sepulchre?—'T is SHE—
'T is *woman*—lovely *woman!* And, in fine,
Wherever PITY dwells, there is HER *home!*

WHO looks on *my* bereavements? and *who* feels
(I mean, *who feels*, in sober seriousness;
For, the mere *name* of proffered sympathy
I little value:)—I repeat, *who* feels
With me, and *for* me, while I weep—ALONE?
Who?—Woman, lovely woman. Lordly man
Perhaps will deign a "look;" then with the "priest
And Levite, on the other side pass by."
Who's the "Samaritan," with "oil and wine?"—
'T is *Woman*, lovely *Woman*—"*A. E. M.*"
—God bless thee, *lovely one!* for thou canst *feel!*

Once and again I've read thy touching lines:—
Again tears flow unbidden!—well they know
Their wonted channel; and their fountain-head
Would seem exhaustless; else their ceaseless streams,
Full and o'erflowing for so many years,
Must have exsiccated their briny source.
Thy record is my witness. Thou hast seen
"Grief's bitter tears bedew my pallid cheek;
And mark'd the deep emotions of my breast,
Until thy heart has been too full for utterance!"

Here, then, in woman's heart I find a balm—
A sterling sympathy—pure "oil and wine"
Poured freely, copiously, into the "wound"
That festers in mine heart! Here, all that love
Or sympathy can do, to cicatrize
The wound of bleeding sensibility,
Is generously accorded. And, I own,
A joy is felt; a calm but seldom found:
But no true peace, no lasting joy is mine,
Till my "form rests beneath the grass-green sod;"
For death alone can give this heart repose!

Well pleased, I "wake again my mournful lyre"
At thy request; and I rejoice to learn
"Its plaintive minstrelsy is sweet, and thrills
With pleasure on thine ear." Its tones indeed
Are plaintive; for I long have swept its chords

In sorrow's mood; and with a feeble hand
Have poured its strains threnodial. But soon
My tuneless lyre will cease its plaintive lays,
And sink with me in *Lethe's* silent stream.

Thus far I egotize. And now, for *thee*—
My friend—my soother—help-meet in distress—
In misery my companion—only one,
"Through suffering made perfect," duly meet
To succour the distressed:—what shall I say
Of thee, *thou stricken, disappointed one?*
—Even sympathy itself, consigned to words,—
Even consolation's most assuasive voice,
Must ope thy wounds afresh—thy griefs renew!
Thy wrongs, thy injuries, I would recount;
Thy numerous ills, and pangs *without a name!*
But my pen falters, ere I make the attempt.

I feel, indeed, my mind by thine illumed,
And recognise, with thankfulness, the aid:
For, when my genius flags, and that obtuseness
Inherent in the mind, retards my flight,
I re-peruse thy thoughts; and, as old *Dion*
Caught inspiration from the works of *Plato*,
I catch the spark; thy inspiration own;
In tuneful cadence and mellifluent tone,
With an electrick impulse soar away;
And, as by magick, flows the genial lay!

Still, the deep theme transcends my feeble powers ;—
Thy graphick powers alone, can paint the scene!
—Oh, for the potent lyre of Israel's king
To calm the soul's emotion! Oh, for powers
To pour the strain of heavenly joy and peace!

Mysterious, strange, beyond conception dark,
Inscrŭtable and intricate to man,
The ways of the ETERNAL!—Virtue weeps;
Worth lies neglected; Piety is scorned;
Religion outraged; Gratitude repaid
With impious ingratitude, and Love
With hate rewarded; Confidence abused;
And holy Patriotism, neglected, dies!
The Widow's moan is uttered to the wind;
The orphan's tears fall on a sterile soil;
Vice stalks triumphant; and oppression's chain
Binds Innocence in its resistless thrall!

Here, but in part we see. The day will come
When in Eternity's unclouded light,
The *Throne of Justice* shall, unveiled, appear,
And vindicate, to an assembled world,
God's righteous dealings with our erring race.

Cast we our burdens, then, upon the Lord:—
Come with me, my *Elvira!* Come to Christ:
He waiteth to be gracious. But full well
Thou know'st his precious Love, and needest not
Be taught of me; for thou thyself, erewhile,

Hast been my teacher; I, thy docile child.
Yet this exhaustless theme may fill our hearts,
And yield instruction;—each may profit each,
By frequent converse, and "stir up our minds
By putting in remembrance." Bear with me,
Thou faithful follower of the bleeding Lamb!
And let me tell of *Jesus'* matchless Love.
—This is the "Balm in Gilead;" *Christ* himself
The great "Physician," who alone can heal.

Without this precious balm, without the hope
Which *Jesus'* Love inspires,—how dreary all!
How insupportable the numerous ills
Which flesh is heir to! What impervious gloom
Would shroud the future! Earthly things are vain;
True friends are few and rare; joy, seldom found.
This life is full of promise; but we find
In every stage, how false its promises;—
How prone to disappoint, deceive and blight
Our fond anticipations!—Well may we
Adopt the *Wise Man's* sentiment, and say
"All—all is vanity."

Yes, dearest one,
"The pleasures of this world seem trifling toys."
Yet they were given us by a bounteous hand,
And should be duly prized. "Use, then, this world"
Said Paul, "as not abusing it; for, know
Its fashion soon will pass—soon fade away."
—Well, let it pass away. Thou as myself,

Hast seen its pictured visions mock the sight;
Its pledge of future pleasure, *unredeemed;*
Deceptive all its promises of good.
—On *earth,* let us not lean. Well was it named
"A broken reed, at best, and oft a spear,
On whose sharp point, peace bleeds and hope expires!"

Where is the ark of safety for that wretch,
Who dares reject a *Saviour's* proffered Love?
The heaven-daring Infidel disclaims
The *mystick Son of Mary:* And the "fool
Hath in his heart declared, *there is no God.*"
But let that God,—whose *being* fools deny,
And that blest *Virgin Son,* whom the rash breath
Of infidelity hath mocked,—be thanked
That we believe not so; and that from *such*
He maketh us to differ—for, like theirs,
Blindness had been our lot, had not his grace—
His rich, his sovereign, his preventing grace,
Been made sufficient for our light and guide.

O, then, to boundless Grace, be all the praise!
The grace of Him, whose goodness crowns our days,
His grace—who died a ruined world to save,
Who rose, the "first fruits" of the gloomy grave;
His grace—whose power the stony heart transforms,—
With Love Divine, the insensate bosom warms:—
The grace of God—the Spirit, Father, Son;
The Eternal One in Three, and Three in One!

TRIBUTE OF RESPECT

TO

ANDREW JACKSON,

PRESIDENT OF THE UNITED STATES OF AMERICA.*

A LL hail to the Chieftain—Columbia's Glory!
N o shade on whose 'scutcheon shall ever descend:
D own the long tract of Time, shall thy fame's hallowed
R esplendently shine—till creation shall end! [story

E ncircled with glory, each patriot action,
W hich thy brilliant career has emblazoned in light;—
J urisprudence adorning—and quelling all faction—
A FABIUS in peace, and a CÆSAR in fight!

C olumbia beholds, in her Hero, retiring,
K nown Valour, pure Worth, and stern Virtue long tried;
S o fades on the sight, the last sun-beam, expiring,
O 'er the face of creation, in rich beauties dyed.

N ow sinking to rest, a bright halo of glory
P ours deathless effulgence o'er thy native land,
R eflecting thine Image, in honour grown hoary,
E vincive of strength, while united we stand.

S hall thy *Patriæ Amor*—thy lucid example,
I n peace and in warfare,—the patriot's delight,
D epart with thine exit,—on Liberty trample,—
E mitting no ray, our respect to invite?—

N o: all-coming Time, in his ceaseless rotation,
T hy lessons, instructive, shall pour on the mind
O f millions unborn;—so shall each generation
F eel secure, as thy maxims on free hearts they bind.

T he tongue of detraction, once rife with foul slander,
H ow palsied and mute, as thy wisdom has shone!—
E ach venal defamer, each pitiful pander,
U nheeded and scorned, to oblivion is gone!

N ow thy wisdom, thy firmness, thy virtue united
I nspire every heart with a patriot flame
T o honour the CHIEF, whom our Country invited
E xecutive *Justice* to stamp with THY NAME.

D ominion is odious, and hateful the station,
S wayed by tyranny's scourge, or oppression's fell rod:
T hrice blessed of Heaven is this favour'd Nation,
A t whose helm is a Ruler, confiding in God!

In sorrow's mood; and with a feeble hand
Have poured its strains threnodial. But soon
My tuneless lyre will cease its plaintive lays,
And sink with me in *Lethe's* silent stream.

Thus far I egotize. And now, for *thee*—
My friend—my soother—help-meet in distress—
In misery my companion—only one,
"Through suffering made perfect," duly meet
To succour the distressed:—what shall I say
Of thee, *thou stricken, disappointed one?*
—Even sympathy itself, consigned to words,—
Even consolation's most assuasive voice,
Must ope thy wounds afresh—thy griefs renew!
Thy wrongs, thy injuries, I would recount;
Thy numerous ills, and pangs *without a name!*
But my pen falters, ere I make the attempt.

I feel, indeed, my mind by thine illumed,
And recognise, with thankfulness, the aid:
For, when my genius flags, and that obtuseness
Inherent in the mind, retards my flight,
I re-peruse thy thoughts; and, as old *Dion*
Caught inspiration from the works of *Plato*,
I catch the spark; thy inspiration own;
In tuneful cadence and mellifluent tone,
With an electrick impulse soar away;
And, as by magick, flows the genial lay!

A WELCOME
TO THE
NEW YORK WEEKLY MESSENGER.

Hail! to thee, "Weekly Messenger!"—all hail!
Once more we greet thy *rising into life*
Like Phœnix from its ashes.
For a while
Thou hast reposed—hast slept—perchance hast dreamed;
But, thanks to that vivifick principle
Inherent in thy nature, thou hast come
Again to visit us with radiant smiles.

A deep sepulchral silence long has reigned
Since thy last visit. An *hiatus*, broad
And deep, has intervened, since thy rich page,
Well stored with intellectual food, has blessed
Our longing sight. At stated intervals
We looked for thee, and welcomed the approach
Of our beloved hebdomadal; whose lore,
Of varied order,—Science, Literature,
Religion, Agriculture, Poësy,—
Impressed all hearts; instructed all who read;
And none was found to censure, or condemn.
—Yes, thy renascent life once more we greet:—
Now may'st thou live and thrive. May FOSTER-ing care
Protect, sustain and nourish thy new birth,
And long—oh, long—give thee a name to live!

Remembrance wakes the tear, at Badger's name:—
He was thy *primum mobile*, "lang syne."
His cultivated, classick, pious mind,
Ardent and potent in the cause of truth,

Long o'er thy page, like tutelary saint,
Presided. But, alas! by Heaven's high will,
He was bereft—afflicted—smitten—bruised!
—Where is he now?—we know not where he is;
But as the mantle of Elijah, seer,
On seer Elisha fell; so his descends
On other *seers*, with dignity who wear
His venerated mantle. Minds like his,
Bright with Castalian dew, thy cause espouse;
And kindred hearts with piety imbued,
And warmed alike with pure devotion's flame,
Spread o'er thy page an intellectual feast.

Then, who will not their coadjutors be?—
Come, *Sisters!—Brothers!*—lend a hand with me;
If, haply, we the Editorial toil
May somewhat lighten,—not their lustre soil.
Where is that galaxy of stars, which, erst,
On the beholder's vision, radiant, burst?
Names, both to science and religion, dear,
Whose strains pathetick drew the unbidden tear:
Whose themes didactick held benign control
O'er every heart, and tranquilized each soul.
O, let these twinkling gems a purer ray
Beam in effulgence from their realms of day;
Dispense their mental treasures round the land,
And scatter blessings with a liberal hand;
Illume the mind that o'er these pages pores,
And light the path of him, to Heaven who soars

We cordial hail thee, "MESSENGER," again,
And say—*Esto perpetuum* thy reign!

Mt. Parnassus, Con., April, 1839.

TO MY BROTHER, REV. E. L. B.....;[25]

ON THE SIXTY-FIRST ANNIVERSARY OF HIS BIRTH:—AUG. 20, 1838.

Each year, in its flight, brings a home-felt monition—
Zealously strive your salvation to gain;
Embrace proffered mercy:—whate'er your condition,
King Jesus to save you, on Calvary was slain!

In this precious Saviour, then trust for salvation,—
Escape Satan's bondage,—prepare for the skies:
Lo! rapidly flies our short day of probation,—
Let nothing deter us from seizing the prize.

Youth is past—manhood fleeteth—old age overtakes us;
Serenely we'll wait till the Saviour shall call:—
All praise to Immanuel, whose sacrifice makes us
Not fear to be clad in the shroud and the pall!

Delightful to view, those bright regions of glory,
Enrapturing the vision of Heavenly Light!
REDEMPTION is purchased! O let the glad story
Break over a world, doomed to sin's lurid night!

A day is approaching—the end of all sorrow;
Sin, Death, Hell are vanquished,—the Grave has no chain:
Celestial effulgence illumes that blest morrow—
Oh! swell the loud anthem to JESUS, whose sorrow
Made *mortals* IMMORTAL, and freed us from pain!

SONNET.

INSCRIBED TO MRS. L. A. E. OF PROVIDENCE, R. I.

LIFE's bright illusions, fancy drawn,
 Youth's raptured gaze too oft arrest;
Dreams of delight the scene adorn,
 In fancy's magick beauty dress'd.

As o'er Life's tide we joyous sail,
 A shade of gloom oft clouds the scene;
No pilot's skill can brave the gale,—
 None, but Religion's form serene.

Encircled by her mild control,
 Let ocean-waves thy barque submerge;
Light beams on the despairing soul,—
 IMMANUEL calms the angry surge!
Oh, lean on *Him*, whose arm can save
Thee from the dread o'erwhelming wave.

A TESTIMONIAL OF AFFECTION.

WRITTEN IN THE ALBUM OF MY NEPHEW.[30]

——————————'T is all I claim,
Here to record a Token of my Love
To thee, *sole offspring* of my Sister dear!
Nor needs this Record. For to mine, thy heart
Doth beat responsive!——————

Spirit of the Bless'd!
My loved Almeda! gently hover near!
In this dear youth thy semblance we behold.
Thy dying prayer, fraught with maternal love
And love connubial, high Heaven invoked
To bless thy spouse, "and smile on Edwin too."
Thy prayer was heard. For, here remains thy son,
A monument of mercy and of grace.
—Not unto us, O Lord! not unto us,
But to thy name, be all the glory given!

Still, still Thy grace impart; protect Thy child;
Grant him Thy guidance through this vale of tears;
And in his Saviour's image may he rise
To dwell with Thee above.——————

THE LAST OF HIS FAMILY.

Providence, June 24, 1839.

SONNET.

INSCRIBED TO MRS. D. C.....; OF HARTFORD, CON.

DWELLING on earth, by Heaven's decree,
O may your mind, from error free,
Religion's sacred truths embrace:—
On life's frail barque and stormy sea,
Time soon will end your race!

How blest to view, with tranquil eye,
Yon glorious mansions in the sky,
Celestial visitants that wait;—
Heaven lifts its golden portals high,
And hails your blissful state.

Unchanging love pervades that state,—
No toils of earth, no adverse fate,
Can part you from the Saviour's love:
Escaped from earth—with hope elate—
Youth marks the saints above.

TO MY DAUGHTER,

MRS. E. LOUISA MATHER.

(On her birth-day, Jan. 7.)

I THINK of thee, my Daughter, when morning's earliest ray
Dispels the darkness of the night, and ushers in the day;
For oft, in morn, your cheerful song was wont to greet mine ear,
But now I'm distant far away,—your song no more I hear!

I think of thee, my Daughter, when Sol high noon has gained;
Then, *tyros*, erst, let loose from school—no longer silence reigned;
When, stepping from the Teacher's throne, I took my elbow chair,
And sought my daughters' carolling, to ease my mind of care.

I think of thee, my Daughter, at twilight's peaceful close,—
For then my daily task was done, and welcome was repose:—
I called my daughters round my chair, and waked their vesper song,
Rejoiced their tuneful notes to hear in cadence flow along.

I think of thee, my Daughter, at midnight's silent hour,
When I my nightly vigils keep, and feel devotion's power;
Far, far from my loved family, I call to mind the past,
And pray that Heaven's protecting wing may over them be cast.

I think of thee, my Daughter, through the diurnal round,
For, though in midst of myriads, I still *alone* am found;
All, ***all I love***, are far from me,—and when my labour ends,
I call to mind my daughters' voice—I weep my absent FRIENDS!

I think of thee,—thy little one,—and all my children dear—
Yes—too intensely do I think,—and shed the frequent tear!—
Oh, may I live to see you all, in joy and peace once more,
And meet you all, no more to part, on Canaan's blissful shore.

Baltimore, Jan. 7

THE ALBUM:

LET IT BE PRESERVED FROM DESECRATION.

How oft we find the Album's page
  Disgraced with mean and trifling lays;
Which, nor on youth, nor feeble age,
  Can ev'n reflect the slightest praise.

And oft, too oft, its leaves display
  A vacant mind—a dearth of thought;
Where Science sheds no lucid ray,—
  Where Learning's gem in vain is sought.

This should not be:—for, in this Book
  Of mental treasures, we would find
(When on its page we cast a look)
  Thoughts, that bespeak the heaven-born Mind.

Here, 'thoughts that breathe, and words that burn,
  Which point to duty's path the heart,—
Fain would the friendly eye discern,
  Free from deceit and guileful art.

For, oft the heart is lured astray,
  By Poesy's insidious power;
And doomed, by lawless passion's sway,
  The victim of a thoughtless hour!

Yet this rich Art, with holier aim,
  Can tranquilize the labouring breast,—
Enkindle pure Devotion's flame,
  And train the soul for heavenly rest.

Let low-born thoughts be banished hence,—
  Mildew of youth,—the bane of age;—
Words, void of sentiment and sense,
  Should never stain the ALBUM's page.

But let the chaste, didactick Muse
  Essay her happiest, noblest power;
And with poetick lore infuse
  Thoughts, that will sooth a dying hour!

TO LOUISA.

WRITTEN ON HER BIRTH-DAY.

If e'er thy Friend, by error led,
  Hath filled thy faithful heart with grief,
Oh, let his tears, in sorrow shed,
  Bring to that faithful heart relief:
For, ne'er shall my affection wane,
While I my reasoning powers retain.

The flame, which youthful love inspired,
  Was kindled at Affection's shrine;
What, then, my youthful heart admired
  In thee, is treasured as divine:
And though the clouds of life obscure
Love's lustre,—Love shall still endure.

No marvel, if, while on the road
  Of chequered life, where thorns abound,
Some thorns, our happiness to goad,
  Should in this thorny path be found:
A cordial, still, we keep in view—
Our youthful Love is ever true.

No thorns of earth shall wound our peace,—
That peace which flows from conscious truth;
Which, when all earth's enjoyments cease,
Shall flourish in immortal youth:—
When, in the presence of our Lord,
We find FIDELITY's reward.

Then, to that beatifick state,
Let our united hearts aspire;
Regardless, whether soon or late,
We soar above earth's funeral pyre!
There, in celestial realms of Joy,
May bliss be ours, without alloy.

Mt. Parnassus, Con., Jan. 14.

EULOGIUM

TO THE MEMORY OF A DEAR CHRISTIAN SISTER;

MISS AMANDA ELVIRA MOORE.

[*On receiving a letter from her Mother, giving the particulars of her last illness, and her happy death, at Green Port, July* 27, 1839.]

Jesus wept. Then said the Jews, Behold how he loved him!
St. John, xi. 35, 36.

Thus may our tears, o'er dying friends, laid low
In death's embrace, approved of Jesus, flow.
Then, loved Elvira! o'er thy early bier,
Well may thy kindred shed the friendly tear!
For, round our hearts how was thy life entwined;
How dear—how sacred—was thy spotless mind!
Deep in thy heart reposed that purest gem,
Pearl above price—Religion's diadem.
Whatever station thou wert called to fill,—
Friend, daughter, sister,—shone the Christian still.
Diffusive Love, like Heaven's ethereal breath,
Glowed through thy life, and warmed thy heart in death!
Mild charity through all thy actions ran,
Evincing love to God, and love to man.

Thine the sweet graces which the mind adorn,
Bright as the sparkling lustre of the morn:—
Pervasive light, from science' genial ray,
Poured o'er thy beauteous mind its flood of day;
And plastick art, with her benign control,
Lent her rich aid to beautify thy soul.

Yet all availed not to detain thee here,
And hold thy *Mind* from its congenial sphere.
But long on earth shall thy example shine,
And long thy love shall round our hearts entwine!
Still dost thou speak:—thy form though in the tomb,
Though decked thy Spirit in immortal bloom,—
Still dost thou speak:—thy Christian graces still
Beam on our sight,—with zeal our bosoms fill.
Thy voice harmonious strikes our listening ears,
Inspires our hopes and dissipates our fears.
Thy heavenly precepts, with their sweet control,
Arrest the thoughts, and harmonize the soul.
Thy blest example meets our longing gaze,
And tells—how lovely are RELIGION's ways!
Thy daily walk and converse fancy views,
Which o'er our pathway shed celestial dews:
By night, by day, thy tones we seem to hear,
Which erst in life enchained the ravished ear,—
As thou wert wont to sing IMMANUEL's love,
Warmed by the Holy Spirit—Heavenly Dove—

And bear our raptured souls up Calvary's height,
Till we beheld the blood-stained Cross in sight!
While heavenly pathos warmed thy feeble breast,
As thy sweet notes portrayed the realms of rest!
That dulcet voice now hymns the ceaseless lay
To JESUS' love—in realms of upper day!

We would not disannul that high behest,
Which called thee, *Sister!* to the realms of rest;
Yet can we not restrain the scalding tear,
That flows spontaneous o'er thy early bier:—
No—no, nor *would we*:—Joy we feel in grief,
Joy—that from suffering thou hast found relief.
But, transient are earth's joys!—Then will we bring
To deck thy grave, the earliest flowers of spring;
And o'er thy hallowed dust will yearly strew
The sweetest flowers, impearled with heavenly dew—
The emblem of our tears;—the flowers, of *thee*,
Unsullied—pure—in virgin modesty.
Too pure for earth, thou 'rt summoned to the skies!
Oh, may our SAVIOUR suffer us to rise,
And join, and know thee, on the heavenly plains,
Unite our voices in seraphick strains,
To hymn the praises of redeeming Love,
Which made us meet on earth to join the saints above.

Mt. Parnassus, Con.

To those, who are not strangers to a Father's heart, *no apology is necessary for inserting the following chaste and affectionate lines, recently received from a beloved daughter, some of whose productions the reader has already seen.*

SATURDAY EVENING TWILIGHT.

INSCRIBED TO MY FATHER.

THIS is the hour, dear Father, when our hearts
Mingled in sweet communion: when the hum
And busy labour of the week were o'er,
And we could sit with care-unshadowed brows,
Gazing upon the beautiful: the moon
In her majestick glory, and the stars
With their unsullied beauty. And from them
With joy we turned to *their* great Author, GOD,
Our Father and our Friend, who form'd this earth
So beautiful and glorious. In that hour,
The thrilling musick of our vesper hymn
Came from our household voices; and the one

Most potent to address the wanderer,
And bring him back to virtue and to peace,
Was there with all its magick influence.
It was my *mother's!* Oh, that soothing voice
Will never cease to hover o'er my heart,
Speaking in angel-tones, till memory's sun
Shall set to rise no more! And, Father, yet
The radiance of *thy* smile lingers around
To soften and to bless; and it shall have
A mighty charm to guard me against ill.
My fair-haired sisters, too, and brothers dear,
All claim a fond remembrance, and they have
The fervent blessings of a sister's heart.
Father, thy home is now afar from mine;
Vast waters roll between us: and I have
Dear ties that bind me to *another* home;
Yet, yet my heart retains its love for thee,
And when are past old Jordan's waves, a home
Will then be ours, where parting never comes!

LOUISA.

Millington, Ct.

A TOKEN OF AFFECTIONATE REMEMBRANCE.

FOR MY REVEREND AND MUCH ESTEEMED FRIEND.[37]

On his birth-day.

SHALL thy Friend, once again, on the *ninth of November*,
O'er the past cast a view, and to memory recall
Life's devious maze;—while with joy I remember
Off my youth's lurid morn, thou didst lift the dark pall!
My heart, ever rife with the purest emotion,
Offers freely to thee, its most grateful returns;
Nor, till life's latest hour, will withhold its devotion,
But cherish the flame which so gratefully burns.
Lo! a crown of bright radiance, from heaven descending,
A promised reward in yon orient sphere—
Kindly waits thine approach, from the grave when ascending,
Secured by thy deeds of Beneficence here.
Lorenzo—though wanting thy kindness attending—
Enshrines in his heart all thy worth, while is blending
Each day, with his prayers, holy Gratitude's tear!

Mt. Parnassus, Ct., Nov. 9, 1834.

ON THE FENCE.

I would that thou wert cold or hot. So, then, because thou art lukewarm, and neither cold nor hot, I will spew thee out of my mouth.—REV. III. 15, 16.

HERE let me perch. How blest when such a seat
Is in reserve for US—the *wise*, the *great!*
For who could bear to mingle with the throng
Of such as talk of *conscience!*—a mere song!
Thank heaven, from such annoyance I am free;
Who wish repose, come mount the fence with me.
I view the earth-born race with indignation,
Who pay to PRINCIPLE their adoration.
For what is *principle?*—an empty name!
Conscience and principle are but a shame—
A blot—a stigma:—lay such trash aside,
And if you wish for *fame*, come to the *fence*, and ride!

What numerous topicks set the world ajar!
Temperance and Anti-Slavery, Peace and War,
Colonization, Anti-masonry, Banks:—
And *pseudo Patriots*, of all names and ranks,
Whigs, Federals, Loco-focos, Democrats,
Van Buren-Webster-Clay-and-Jackson-brats,—
All strive alike; and each, to gain his wishes,
Would feast on Whig or Administration "fishes!"

Here, ON THE FENCE, I hold the golden mean,
And scorn in party contests to be seen.
RELIGIOUS PARTIES! How can such endure?
I 've no religion:—*ergo*—I am PURE!
Conscious I am of "absolute volition;"
And, whence derived, affects not my condition.
And whether I'm *impelled* by "moral suasion,"
Or fixed "decree,"—each answers my occasion.
And whether I believe "one God, or twenty,"
Whose business is 't?—sure we have *creeds* in plenty.
Why should I care for others' creeds, I beg;—
"They neither rob my purse, nor break my leg!"[28]
"For modes of faith, let graceless zealots" squabble,
I 'm *on the fence*, and thus keep out o' the hobble!

In all the *moral efforts* of the day,
Does not self-interest hold a ruling sway?
Who, but the man that knows the use of figures
To *compound interest*, cares about the "niggers?"
I care no more about "amalgamation,"
Than its antipodes, "colonization;"
For, is not slavery sanctioned by the law?
Then, why thus rashly brave this lion's paw?
And why should Temperance rouse the world to arms?
For wise men still admit that *rum* has charms!
If no true *courage* we by birth inherit,
Why not *create* some, with New-England spirit?
Yet think not me an advocate for drinking;
"Let it alone"—all will work right, I'm thinking.

Again, what use in Bible-clubs and Missions?
To foster these, we harm our own conditions:—
Who goes on Missions at his own expense?
To lack in *money* argues lack of *sense.*
If we bestow our cash to teach the pagans,
(Ourselves, the while, as ignorant as Mohegans,)
We certainly betray a want of reason;—
To instruct *domestick heathen,* 't is the season.

Why turn our thoughts to "Moral Reformation,"
Although *licentiousness* pervades the nation?
Why hail the *seventh* command, with importunity?
The other NINE are broken with impunity!
This is a land of liberty and law;—
But laws should never hold *free* men in awe!
I am for "let alone;"—on neutral ground;
In HOLY QUARRELS I would ne'er be found.

Here, on my neutral throne, securely seated,
By passing brawlers on each side I 'm greeted,
Doff my *chapeau* to each, with bland palaver,
Trusting to meet, in proper time, their favour.
I watch the wind and tide of popularity,
And view with joy, in *parties,* a disparity;
Ready, when either rules, to quit the fence,
(Sure to be hailed a man of sterling sense,
By *any party* claiming the majority,)
And join with them to slander the minority.

SOLILOQUY.

With all my vaunting, is my mind at rest?
Free from all doubt, with conscious virtue blest?
Can mere *inaction* claim the just applause,
Which those enjoy, who *strive* in Virtue's cause?
For, though on neutral ground, it is my pride,
Religion, truth and conscience to deride;
Yet dread misgivings oft invade my heart,
And *conscience*, GOD's vicegerent, points a dart!
A great FIRST CAUSE 't is impious to deny;—
We read his NAME, on ocean, land and sky.
For nought but power omnifick could combine
These wondrous structures, that in glory shine.
And who shall say the Bible is a lie,
And its behests by human wisdom try?
Or that the holy Gospel is a dream
Of stupid bigots, who but righteous *seem?*
—If, then, its page is stamped with living truth,
To cheer our age, to guide our froward youth;—
If its blest Author was our SAVIOUR—GOD,
How shall weak man brave his avenging rod?
And of these words, who shall endure the sound,
"He, that 's not for me, is against me found!"*
Vain, then, the hope, on *neutral ground* to find
A calm sojourn for the self-conscious mind.

* St. Matt. xii. 30.

As well might doomed PROMETHEUS hope for rest,
With ever-gnawing vulture at his breast!
Too long I 've been *inert* :—life's transient space
Draws to a close!—and, passed, my day of grace!
My footstool 's gone!—my dreams of bliss are o'er!
A soundless gulf!—a sea without a shore!
The dread reality appears in view;
Too late, I own God's holy Word is true;
And well may fear, no fence, or neutral ground,
Is, in the ETERNAL FUTURE, to be found!

FAREWELL TO MOUNT PARNASSUS;

WITH A

VALEDICTORY TO THE MUSES.

Carmina nulla canam—Virgil.

There is a magick charm steals o'er the heart,
As we review the past:—and round the spot,
Which long hath borne the sacred name of home,
Cluster the best affections of the soul!
And when that spot we leave, the mind still dwells
A willing captive there.

The thoughts revert
With pleasure to that holy household shrine,
Where incense, morn and eve, was wont to rise
From hearts imbued with piety and love
To Him who gives us all. The name of home—
That sacred name—how dear! Connubial love
Holds foremost rank in sweet affection's chain;
Parental fondness next; then filial piety;
And love fraternal crowns the circling joy!

Such scenes of dear delight I long have known,
Such charms have felt, such joys have shared, on thee,
My loved PARNASSUS! But the time *must* come,
Which mars all earthly joys—which sunders ties
Most dear—too dear, for human happiness.
—There, on that classick Mount, for seventeen years,
Indulgent Heaven hath nurtured me, and mine.
There, hath the ORPHAN INVALID reposed,
And shared, in good degree, the gifts which God
In rich profusion pours on erring man.
There, drew my children breath:—there formed their minds
From Academus' rich and sapient fount.
There, my loved daughters other arms embraced,
And from my fostering umbrage bore them thence.
And there—which adds a pang to my remove—
There, now I leave them, near that rural Mount,
My favourite PARNASSUS.—And thou Hill—
Namesake of one, well known in classick lore—
Thee, with my daughters, now I bid adieu,
And you, my neighbours—friends—acquaintance—all,
And far away to "Penn's thronged city" hie.

And live there those, who breathe for me a prayer
Fraught with benevolence? Does friendship's voice
Pursue my steps, invoking benisons
On the lone orphan, and his little band?
—Yes, the delightful thought I will indulge,
That bosoms, warm with friendship's sacred flame,

Are there, which beat in unison with mine.
Bear with me, friends :—why should it not be so?
In joy and sorrow I have sympathized
With some of you ;—around the dying couch
I've ministered ; and with these feeble lungs
Performed the last sad office o'er your DEAD :—
Have led your youth in science' flowery walks,
And striv'n to train their nascent minds for heaven.
And some of these—my witnesses—remain :
And other some have entered on the stage,
In life's eventful *drama*, to perform
The various several parts to each assigned.
Some in the Forum—in the sacred Desk—
And some in halls of Legislation placed,
"Of patriot eloquence to flash down fire
Upon their country's foes ;"—salvation's light
To pour on death's dark valley, and restore
The privileges of the sons of God
To souls by sin enslaved ;—the cause to plead
Of widows—orphans—injured Innocence—
And gain redress for those by wrong oppressed.
While others, in the self-denying task
'To teach the young idea how to shoot,'
And train for usefulness the infant mind,
Though in a sphere unhonoured by the world—
Enjoy the *luxury of doing good.*
Thus, in life's varied scenes all act their part.
Where are the hoary heads which crowned that Mount

When first I came?—'Our fathers—where are they?'
They lie 'beneath the long luxuriant sod!'

The frosts of age begin to blanch my locks,
As now I take my exodus from you,
And me premonish—*I must soon lie low.*
But youthful vigour nerves my feeble frame,
And pristine friendly feeling warms my heart,
While I thus bid you all a sad *Adieu:*

"Farewell, my friends!—farewell, my foes!
My peace with *these,*—my love with *those*:—
One friendly wish, one fervent prayer,
I breathe for every creature there."

And while I bid that classick mount, Adieu,
And seek, far off, a more congenial clime;
Let my Farewell embrace the Muses, too,
No more to woo them—through all coming time.

Yet, from you, lovely Nymphs! with grief I part;
For, long your magick spell, around me thrown,
Hath filled with hope this desolated heart,
That ye your faithful votary would own.

I've wooed you long, in Academus' bowers,—
Lyceum's walks,—at Heliconia's fount;
I've strewed my pathway with your richest flowers,
And, 'mid your smiles, have scaled Parnassus' Mount.

—And YE *have owned me* :—mine has been the meed,
  A guerdon rich, in your bright smiles to bask ;
In groves—by streams—along the flowery mead—
  In sweets I revell'd, while I plied my task.

But life declines :—no longer I aspire
  To poet's honours,—nor of fame I dream ;
My tuneless harp and my discordant lyre
  Returnless sink in LETHE's silent stream.

FAREWELL.

F AREWELL ! how that word thrills the heart with emotion,
A nd recalls to the mind Joys no more to return ;
R eviving those scenes, where the heart's pure devotion
E nkindled a flame, that must ceaselessly burn !
W hat though it is uttered—can time's separation
E ffiace from the memory the joys of the past ?
L o ! a bliss is in prospect, for whose preparation
L ife's day is well spent, if we reach it at last.

NOTES.

Note 1, page 10.

> See—see, removed to yonder sea-girt Isle,
> One lovely *Flower*—

Elvira, the first victim of *consumption* in my father's house, spent a summer in the family of our maternal uncle, the Rev. EMERSON FOSTER, Pastor of the church at Oyster Ponds, now Green Port, Long Island, in the hope of finding relief in a milder climate. Though her disease was somewhat mitigated, she derived no real benefit from a change of climate, but evidently declined; as was evinced by the impression, which her death-like appearance made on her father, at his first interview, when he went to conduct her home.

Note 2, page 58.

> ——tell how my *Sister* pined.

See the above note. The friends, to whom this poem was addressed, were descendants of the uncle above named, who himself had been long dead; and of whose family I had for many years had no intelligence.

Note 3, page 62.

Elvira. One of the friends, described in the preceding note;—grand-daughter of the Rev. *Emerson Foster*.

Note 4, page 71.

> The Friend of man, see WORCESTER rise.

The Rev. *Noah Worcester*, D. D. of Brighton, Mass., now deceased; author of "A solemn review of the custom of War;" a philanthropist, and an able and successful champion of the cause of universal Peace. He was the founder of the "Massachusetts Peace Society;" and, at his suggestion, the author was the first mover in forming a Peace Society in Connecticut; and by the blessing of God, was successful in founding the "East-Haddam Branch of the Massachusetts Peace Society," Dec. 1818; the anniversary of which was observed for seventeen years.

Note 5, page 76.

Laus Spiritui Sancto. PRAISE TO THE HOLY SPIRIT.

Note 6, page 82.

See nought beyond, but plains that meet the skies.

In the far distant horizon, the land and sky *appear* to meet.

Note 7, page 83.

And like *Prometheus'* vulture rest denies.

Classical allusion.—"Jupiter being angry at *Prometheus*, for stealing fire from heaven, sent Mercury to chain him to Mount Caucasus, and to set a vulture to gnaw his liver, which grew again as fast as it was devoured!"

Note 8, page 88.

On inserting this poem in his paper, the Editor of the N. Y. Weekly Messenger, prefaced it with these very courteous remarks:—"It is a pleasant duty for the Editor of the Messenger to call attention to the following poetick effusion. The subject on which our correspondent writes, is one worthy of his genius—one that merits the exercise of his noblest powers. Few evils of that character, are more in need of correction, than the morbid taste which exists among our fair countrywomen, for the "stale, flat, and unprofitable" crudities, which so often soil the pages of Albums."

Note 9, page 101.

Mt. Parnassus :—A classick name, by which that eminence was known, whereon was the author's residence in Connecticut.

Note 10, page 104.

A disease, similar to the *small-pox*, mysteriously entered the village of Chester, where she was then residing, and suddenly snatched her from the world.

Note 11, page 1.

Her elder sister was attacked with the same disease, and brought near the grave; but through God's mercy was restored. Thus was "the one taken, and the other left:" which was beautifully illustrated in a solemn and impressive discourse by the Rev. *Isaac Parsons*, from St. Matt. xxiv. 40, on the Sunday after the interment of the deceased.

Note 12, page 130.

——————came *Magdalene* forth.

Although this name is more commonly pronounced in three syllables, it is necessary in poetry to adhere to the classick pronunciation—*Mag-da-le′-ne.* I have, however, often witnessed this pronunciation of it, by some of our most accomplished scholars, in in reading the scriptures. This is doubtless a correct pronunciation of the word: and in like manner are pronounced the names of the Muses—*Mel-pom′-e-ne, Cal-li′-o-pe, Terp-si-cho′-re,* &c. The restraints of poetry sometimes oblige us to violate the rules of just pronunciation. Of this, the author was conscious, in the use of the Latin word *Manes,* in the first poem in this volume, and also page 100, where we are obliged to utter the word in one syllable, instead of two as required by the Latin idiom.

Note 13, page 135.

——————with bold *Icarean* flight.

Classical allusion.—"*Icarus,* the son of Daedalus, flying with his father from Crete with artificial wings, and soaring *too high,* the sun melted his waxen pinions; and he fell into that part of the sea between Mycone and Gyaros, which from him was called the *Icarean sea.*"

Note 14, page 145.

"The following beautiful poetick effusion—which we copy from the Hartford Review—is, we suspect, from the pen of one who has, much to our gratification, occasionally favoured us with the labours of his leisure moments."—Editor *of the Sentinel and Witness, Middletown, Con.*

Note 15, page 168.

This poem was elicited, by noticing in the New York Weekly Messenger,—for the columns of which the author had frequently contributed,—the following inquiry:—"What has become of our friend and correspondent, N. L. F.? We hope he has not forgotten us."—And, on inserting the poem in his paper, the talented Editor, Mr. Badger, introduces it with this complimentary caption:—

"We *must* recommend the following production to the careful perusal of our patrons. We have been greatly amused by its reading. There is a strain of excellent good humour throughout the first part; which has tended, in no small degree, to awaken our risible faculties. So, it appears, if we may judge from the *chilly* tone of our good friend, that the reason why we have not heard from him in so long a time, may be attributed to the severity of the weather. Really, the winters are getting to be serious, to "*freeze up*" our very poets!—'What is the country coming to?'"

Note 16, page 173.

Allusion is here made to the destructive fire in New York; Dec. 16, 1835.

Note 17, page 175.

Written in the unusually *cold spring*, of 1836.

Note 18, page 175.

Alluding to "THE GREAT HERSCHEL DISCOVERIES;" a finished *Hoax*, by that graphick writer and able Editor, R. A. LOCKE, Esq.

Note 19, page 179.

Perhaps a more dastardly, and at the same time, a more permanent and enduring wrong, was never done to one individual by another, than that which was effected by *Americus Vespucius* to the injury of COLUMBUS, in insidiously supplanting him in giving a NAME to this continent. Says that classick and energetick writer, DR. MORSE—"The bold pretensions of a fortunate impostor have robbed the discoverer of the New World of a distinction that belonged to him. The name of *Americus* has supplanted that of COLUMBUS; and mankind are left to *regret an act of injustice, which, having been sanctioned by time, they can never redress.*"

Note 20, page 180.

The variation of the Magnetick Needle.

Note 21, page 182.

Ferdinand Columbus tells us, that his Father kept the FETTERS, in which he was brought home, hanging up in an apartment of his house, as a perpetual memorial of *national ingratitude;* and when he died, ordered them to be buried in the same grave with himself.

Note 22, page 183.

"Americus Vespucius, a Florentine gentleman, accompanied Ojeda, an enterprising Spanish adventurer, to America; and having, with much art, and some degree of elegance, drawn up an amusing history of his voyage, he published it to the world. It circulated rapidly, and was read with admiration. In his narrative, he had insinuated that the glory of having first discovered the New World, belonged to him. This was in part believed, and the country began to be called after the name of its supposed first discoverer. The unaccountable caprice of mankind has perpetuated the error; so that now, by the universal consent of all nations, this new quarter of the globe is called AMERICA."—DR. MORSE.

Note 23, page 186.

This was written in reply to a poem by "A. E. M." entitled "The Voice of Friendship;" inscribed to the author, and published in the N. Y. Weekly Messenger. She was a pious, devoted and consistent *sister*, of the Church of CHRIST.

Note 24, page 193.

If this tribute to GEN. JACKSON shall be found obnoxious to the displeasure of his political opponents; or, if even his friends should deem it too high an eulogium;—the author (who is, and ever has been, a *Federal Republican*,) respectfully requests his readers, of every political party, candidly to bear in mind the *Poet's license*. This "Tribute" was originally sent to Gen. JACKSON, in manuscript, at the time of its date; and was responded to in a very polite and complimentary letter from under the General's own hand.

Note 25, page 198.

My brother-in-law, *Lysander;* the husband of *Elvira*.—See, first note.—Rev. EZEKIEL LYSANDER BASCOM, died at Fitzwilliam, N. H., April 2, 1841. Æ. 64.—"Calmly and prayerfully, he fell asleep in JESUS."

Note 26, page 200.

The only child of *Almeda*, my youngest sister. See the first poem.

Note 27, page 213.

Rev. SOLOMON BLAKSLEE; first Rector of St. Stephen's, East Haddam, Con.; subsequently, Rector of St. James', New London:—since, deceased at Butternuts, N. Y.—See, also, page 36.

Note 28, page 215.

"What need I care, whether my neighbour believes in one God, or twenty Gods?—it neither picks my pocket, nor breaks my leg."—JEFFERSON.

THE END.

www.ingramcontent.com/pod-product-compliance
Lightning Source LLC
LaVergne TN
LVHW050527100826
845148LV00002B/465

* 9 7 8 1 4 2 5 5 2 0 1 2 0 *